I've known Sandi for more than a quarter of a century. I'm one of the millions who have been blessed by her voice and touched by her words of wisdom. Her story is one of grace, hope, and second chances. May it impact all who read it.

—Max Lucado, pastor; author, *Unshakable Hope*

That voice! I'm talking about the voice of Sandi's heart—the voice that invites us into her struggles and allows all of us to see part of our own story in hers. I'm talking about the voice that is constantly championing others and making them feel seen, valued, and heard. This book will help restore the voices of so many who feel sidelined and silenced.

—Natalie Grant, singer

I've known Sandi ever since she was a kid singing backup at our studio. I've always loved her talent, her energy, and her heart. This refreshingly honest account of her story sets a remarkable example for anyone who wants his or her voice to make an eternal difference in this world.

—Bill Gaither, singer

I love Sandi's voice, her heart, and her passion for Christ. I was deeply moved by the transparency of this book. She shares her journey at a depth that few are brave enough to offer. So find a quiet place and sit with her story for a while. Perhaps you too will find your voice.

—Sheila Walsh, author, *It's Okay Not to Be Okay*

My favorite kind of spiritual leader is the one who tells the truth and gives others permission to tell the truth. I don't need shiny, polished, or tidy. I need genuine. Sandi, my dear friend, whom I love wholeheartedly, has given us this and more in *The Voice*.

—Jen Hatmaker, author; speaker; cofounder, Legacy Collective

I have a voice. It's high pitched, a bit nasal, and as country as cornbread, but it has taken me to places I never dreamed I could go as a comedian. But Sandi is more than just an amazing voice; she is a friend, a mentor, a teacher. This book moved me, challenged me, changed me, and my heart and voice are much improved having traversed these pages with Sandi.

—Chonda Pierce, comedian

I'm so proud of Sandi for having the courage to share the truth about her life and how hearing God's voice helped her discover her own. This book will encourage and inspire you to find your voice as you pursue the dreams and desires God has put in your heart.

—**Robert Morris**, founding senior pastor,
Gateway Church; author, *The Blessed Life*

As I read this book, I realized how hard Sandi has fought against circumstances and experiences that could have silenced her, and it made me respect her even more. She has done what she does best: welcome others to listen to her voice and find their own as they do.

—**Angie Smith**, speaker; author, *Seamless, What Women Fear*

Sandi is gifting us with an encore performance. Sharing wisdom from the latest third of her life, she is candid about the complexity of her journey and the depth of her faith, and we are once again encouraged, strengthened, and made aware of God's love for us all.

—**Suzanne Stabile**, author, *The Path between Us*

Sandi's voice has filled arenas, stadiums, concert halls, and, most important, hearts. The only thing that exceeds her voice is her generous hospitality. When you open the cover of this book, you will feel seen and heard. Welcome to The Voice.

—**Patsy Clairmont**, *You Are More Than You Know*

Sandi wraps real life and raw courage around the exhortation in Proverbs 31:8 to speak up for the voiceless. Her heartwrenching yet redemptive story is infused with the living hope and joy of Jesus Christ, which has the power to make even the driest bones dance!

—**Lisa Harper**, bestselling author and Bible teacher

Spend some time around Sandi and it is easy to forget all the trappings of her fame. She is a grace-filled grace giver. She has much to say that we all need to hear. I've been waiting for this book for a long time. You may not realize it, but you have too.

—**Marty Grubbs**, senior pastor, Crossings Community Church

THE VOICE

Listening for God's Voice
and Finding Your Own

Sandi Patty

with Cindy Lambert

ZONDERVAN

The Voice
Copyright © 2018 by Sandi Patty

Requests for information should be addressed to:
Zondervan, *3900 Sparks Dr. SE, Grand Rapids, Michigan 49546*

ISBN 978-0-310-35233-4 (hardcover)

ISBN 978-0-310-35593-9 (special edition)

ISBN 978-0-310-35237-2 (audio)

ISBN 978-0-310-35235-8 (ebook)

Author is represented by the literary agency of The Fedd Agency, Inc., P.O. Box
341973, Austin, Texas 78734.

Art Direction: Belinda Bass
Cover design: Kristen Ingebretson
Cover photo: Angela Talley
Interior design: Kait Lamphere

First printing August 2018 / Printed in the United States of America

To those who have felt voiceless,
and to those who have been our champions.
And to my family, Don, Anna, Collin, Thatcher,
Madeleine, Jon, Rachel, Jenn, Scott, Aiden, Donnie,
Katie, Aly, Will, Erin, Mollie, Sam, and my parents Ron
and Carolyn Patty, who have helped me find mine.

Contents

Foreword

I first heard "The Voice" so many years ago I can't even remember the date. But I do remember thinking, *Okay, that's a once-in-a-generation kind of talent. That's like a Streisand. God doesn't give that kind of gift very often.* Of course, the voice belonged to Sandi Patty, a young woman destined for greatness. All I know is that she became a lifetime friend.

What you are about to discover about Sandi in this book will shock you, upset you, and ultimately make you rejoice in the power of a life lived well with God.

I had no idea she went through what she describes in this book. She never let on; she never hinted to me that anything was wrong. It remained hidden, painful. She just kept singing with that extraordinary, angelic, powerful, ethereal instrument that defied gravity.

It always sounded effortless to me, like all she had to do was show up, breathe, and open her mouth and the voice would ring out. But what you will discover within these pages is that it was anything but effortless. It was painful and complicated and layered with years of shame.

Sandi's story is one of deep suffering that even those closest to her never fathomed. I am so happy that this extraordinary woman is finally able to tell her story full throttle and unafraid.

"The Voice" has been freed to soar on the wings of the wind the way God, her creator, always planned. But oh, what a long, long time it has taken.

—Kathie Lee Gifford

Prologue

For much of my life, I felt voiceless.

I know those aren't the words one expects to hear from a vocalist with forty Dove awards and more than thirty albums who has spent the better part of four decades singing for a living. That's because I'm not talking about my singing voice. From my earliest memories, singing came as easily and naturally to me as breathing. What didn't come naturally was using my own words to speak my thoughts and feelings, to express my identity—my opinions and value and worth and understanding—to others or even to myself.

If you sense a major disconnect of that description from the woman who eagerly bounds onto the stage and steps into the spotlight, mic in hand, to sing her heart out, you are right. There was a disconnect deep in my spirit.

Shy. Introverted. Sure, those words applied to me, but I'm talking here about something that went far deeper than that. It wasn't just that I kept my thoughts to myself. When it came to my inner life, I struggled against a stranglehold that kept me, the real me, under lock and key, hidden away in shadows so dark I couldn't even see myself, much less speak up to find the help and camaraderie and love I desperately needed.

In the early days of my career, one audience favorite I often performed was an amusing medley of "Jesus Loves Me" that offered a tour through the many phases of developing my style as a musical entertainer. I'd begin by playfully mimicking my voice as a preschooler singing "Jesus Loves Me," then progress to my elementary days of learning to play the song on piano, first with one hand, then with two. The audience would always laugh along as I dramatized my less than fluid renditions.

Then I'd leap forward in time to my days as a high school sophomore who adored Karen Carpenter. Then, to the applause of the crowd, I would sing the familiar song in the style of the famous alto pop star. I'd joke about how when I reached the mature stage of a high school senior, I'd graduated to the elegant style of Barbra Streisand. The crowd always ate it up, whistling and cheering as I concluded the medley with an exaggerated performance of the childhood song in my "serious music" college operatic style. It was a crowd pleaser that I performed simply for fun.

But it's also a picture of Sandi Patty in search of a voice, trying on the voices of others, one after another, hoping to finally find her own. The good news is that in the same way that the fun little medley had a happy ending with my going on to give full concerts in what is very much my own singing voice, I've finally found my inner voice and am learning to speak with it.

I love the encouragement Psalm 116:1 gives: "I love the LORD, for he heard my voice; he heard my cry for mercy."

God heard my voice even when I couldn't hear it myself, and then his voice broke through my walls and shame and wounds and insecurities and self-doubts. He pried away the stranglehold they had on my voice and unleashed me to appreciate and express who he designed me to be.

I am voiceless no more!

And that is why I am writing this book.

I've been on a tremendous journey of discovery, a journey that I now feel compelled to share with all the others who, for a host of reasons, struggle with a voicelessness of their own. Once I began sharing my journey, I discovered I was far from alone. People—men and women alike—have whispered to me about the shadows in their own lives that have kept them feeling shut down and closed off. Because I discovered a secret too important to keep to myself, I want to do what I can to help others open the floodgates of their voices. If we listen for God's voice singing into our lives, we will discover the marvelous voice he has designed for each of us.

Listen with me for God's voice amid the highs and lows, the joys and tragedies of my life and yours.

CHAPTER ONE

The Shy Girl with a Song

"You were only two and a half the first time you sang a solo," Dad said, beaming. It's a story I remember hearing more than once when I was a little girl. I don't remember the solo, but I've seen pictures and heard the story told so many times over the years that it seems embedded in my memory somewhere. I do remember never feeling nervous about singing—whether it was by myself or in front of people. Music was simply the language my family spoke, and I was fluent in it.

My parents have always been musical, and so music was a language that, honestly, I thought every family spoke. My dad was a minister of music for all of the years I can remember. This made me and my two brothers pastor's kids. My mother is an incredible musician and pianist. We would sing around the house, sing in church, and sing in our big wood-paneled station wagon, whether on short trips or long. And if we weren't singing a cappella, the radio would be on and we would sing along.

I remember that sometimes my dad—especially on long trips—found the only radio station available. Classical! Eek. My two younger brothers, Mike and Craig, and I would at first roll our eyes until our dad began to make up stories based on how the music sounded. If the music was quiet and reflective, we heard stories about lost dogs. If the music was big and gallant, we heard stories of heroes and ladies being rescued from the dragon's snare. Music was all around us. It wasn't until a few years later in elementary school that I understood that not every family spoke this language. Ours was special.

Music was woven into the fabric of our family right along with faith. Most of what I knew and understood about God, as a child, came from the songs we sang. I believe you could say that it was through music that I heard the voice of God. From "Jesus Loves Me" to "He's Got the Whole World in His Hands" to "This Little Light of Mine," I learned of God's love and his power and his place in my life.

When I was born, my dad was pastoring in Oklahoma City. Then in 1959, when I was three, he was offered a church position in Phoenix, Arizona. It is of the Phoenix years that I have some of the sweetest memories of music becoming the cornerstone in my life. I had an incredible elementary music teacher named Mrs. Pat Rabe (pronounced Robbie) who brought such fun to music along with giving us a wonderful education. She nudged me forward in my musical education by choosing me to accompany the choir from time to time. And she nudged me forward in my ear training and sightsinging as well. I had no idea that was what she was doing at the time because she made class so fun; it didn't seem like learning. She is the single greatest reason I've always wanted to be a music teacher.

During those Phoenix years, my mother often organized the music for women's events at the church. She was the music pastor's wife, so it was kind of expected, but she didn't mind a bit. (They got two music ministers for the price of one, which was all too common in those days.) One year, for the annual mother-daughter banquet, my mom asked me (I think I was four) if I would do a special song where she would play and I would sing.

"Of course," I said, in whatever way a four-year-old says "of course." My mom had put together a little three-song medley that had to do with spring and rain.

When I was recalling this on the phone with my mom, she said, "We even had costume changes." That cracked me up. The last song in the medley was "Singin' in the Rain," and I wore a little yellow plastic raincoat and held one of those clear plastic umbrellas. My mom played the piano and I sang because that's just what our family did.

Mysterious Applause

My dad began teaching at Phoenix Christian High School when I was about five. He directed the band and the choir, in addition to being the music pastor at First Church of God. The band rehearsed on the football field early in the morning before school started. Let me just say right here that neither my dad nor I are morning people. To this day, if we see 5:00 or 6:00 a.m., it's usually because we've stayed up all night (or I have an early flight), never because we have chosen to wake up that early. But I digress. Along with the marching band, there were the majorettes. Let's just have a moment of awe right here. *The majorettes!* Do you feel me? These lovely young women marched in front of the band in awesome uniforms and had batons they twirled and threw into the air and, to my five-year-old amazement, caught. If you were born in the fifties, you totally know what I'm saying.

One morning, my dad asked me if I wanted to go with him to band practice; he would bring me home after that. (I didn't go to kindergarten because it wasn't required back then.) So, sure, how fun would that be to go to practice with my dad? When I got there, I was excited to meet the majorettes, and they were so nice to me. They asked if I had ever twirled a baton, and I said no, so they showed me how, and I learned pretty quickly. I kept asking Dad if I could keep going with him to band practice, and he kept saying yes, so several mornings each week, this was our thing. My parents even got me my own baton. I felt like such a big girl.

One day my dad announced that the band was going to march at the upcoming football game and asked if I would like to march with the majorettes. Say what? Like, be a majorette? When he told me that it was the majorettes who asked for me, my heart soared. And as though my mother was reading my mind, she told me that she had already bought me a little white pleated skirt, a white turtleneck sweater, and white shoes and socks.

Oddly enough, I didn't take into account that there would be people in the stands watching the band march during halftime. I just found it exciting that we—the band, the majorettes, and me—were going to do what we had done every morning for the past several weeks, but this time, during halftime of a real football game! Halftime arrived and here we came—march, two, three, four, march, two, three, four—around the running track that circled the field. Then one of the majorettes threw her baton into the air and caught it. Super cool.

She then said to me, "Go ahead. Throw it." So I threw my baton and caught it while I kept marching. Understanding how to move with the music and march in time came as naturally to me as singing. I heard off in what seemed like the distance people clap and cheer, but I didn't think much of it the first time. We marched some more; I threw my baton again and caught it. And weird as it seemed, at the same time I caught my baton, I heard clapping and cheering. It struck me as kind of odd that their clapping was timed with my catching. How did that happen? But I had a job to do and formations to make on the football field with the rest of the band, so on I went.

The band performed, and everyone was so happy. The crowd was happy; the school was happy. My dad was happy, and people were shaking his hand because they had never had a band that marched and made formations before.

On the way home, I said to my dad (and I promise you I said this as innocently as it sounds), "Dad, didn't you think it was weird that the crowd clapped at exactly the same time that I caught the baton?"

He puzzled a moment and asked me what I meant.

"How did they know to all clap together then?" I asked.

My dad just grinned and said, "Sandy [yes, the spelling was different—with a *y*—from birth through fifth grade, but that's for another chapter], honey, they were clapping for *you*."

"What?" I said. "Why would they clap for me?"

"Honey, they saw how well you threw your baton and caught it, and they were so happy for you. They wanted you to know that you made them happy, so they were clapping *for you*." I honestly just didn't get it. (I'm not making this up.) Why would someone clap for something I did every day just because I liked doing it? It seemed to be a whole lot bigger deal to everyone else than it was to me. It was just what I did. If people wanted to watch—fine. But I really didn't do it for *them*. I did it because I loved it and it brought me joy.

A Unique Gift

I think those last couple of sentences are the lens through which I have always seen my career. Whether I was singing in my bedroom by myself with my little 45 rpm record player, using my hairbrush as a microphone, or I was singing to eighteen thousand people in a concert with a real microphone, it has all come from the same place. In music, I hear the voice of God and respond to him.

Singing was always so natural to me that when I had to begin to *talk* in school, with teachers or with friends, I didn't know how. I probably presented a more confident affect than I actually felt. Every time I had to put things into words, I cringed inside. Although I liked to read, I was a slow reader. And my comprehension of what I read was slower still. But I liked to understand what I was reading.

Whenever the teacher asked each student to take a section and read out loud, I froze inside. Are you kidding me? This was one of my worst fears. I would stumble through the words, and when I sat down, the teacher would say, "So, Sandy, can you tell us what those words mean?"

Inside I was thinking, *Actually, no. No, I cannot. I have no idea. I have no idea who Jane and Dick are, and I have no idea why they are washing a dog.* But I stumbled and bumbled my way through a somewhat plausible explanation until, thankfully, it was the next student's turn. There were kids in my class who read so fast I realized if I read as fast as they, I could never understand the meaning.

On the other hand, when it came to the principal or the music teacher asking the students whether anyone would volunteer to sing the national anthem for the parent assembly, my hand was up in a shot with an "oh yes" on my tongue. Finally, something I *could* do. I never said it in an arrogant way. I thought, *I hope if I volunteer for this, I don't have to volunteer to make some stupid volcano for the science fair or read to some of the younger students.*

I suppose you could say that music has *always* been my voice. Music let me sing songs, like the one from *The Sound of Music* (when I was feeling a great lack of confidence), "I Have Confidence." I remember thinking, *If I can sing it, I can feel it. And if I can feel it, I can be it.* Even though I had an incredible shyness with spoken words, music helped me speak. Music and lyrics were the voice of my emotions. They expressed my heart's desires, longings, hurts, and questions I could not speak in words. Now all these years later, I've finally uncovered my real, authentic voice. The voice that can also speak words when needed.

The truth is not everyone can sing and understand music. For some, it is hard. But that's okay. You don't have to sing or understand music. I believe that God draws our hearts to the gift he has given us. For me, it's the language of music. To those who love to do detail work, God has gifted you with that. And I can assure you he has not gifted me that way. So I applaud you. And I'm slightly envious of your gift. Those of you who are athletically inclined or who have an empathetic nature, those are God's gifts to you. Become better skilled in your gift. Persevere in it just as Hebrews 12:1 says: "Let us run with perseverance the race marked out for us." God put the joy in our hearts for certain things. And he made us to use the gifts he's given us. Don't back away. Lean in. Become the best *you* that God always intended you to be.

I understand something today about the shy girl and the song. It was really okay for me to be shy with words. No one has every gift. And I've been able to understand that having music and singing as my first voice wasn't a defective setting. They weren't a *less than* setting because I couldn't do other things. Music and singing are *my* setting. It's how God made me. He put the song in my heart. He gave me the voice to sing. I used to think that because singing came more easily to me than other things, it really wasn't important.

I want to encourage you not to overlook the things you are drawn to or the things that come more easily than others. Popular "wisdom" says that if something brings you joy, you are not serving God. It's almost as though we are serving God only when we are miserable. So not true! I think many things that bring us joy are gifts that God gives us to joyfully share with others. They aren't defects. They are divine! They are foundational parts of the *voice* God put within us. May we never overlook the divine in the simplicities that come our way each day.

One of my favorite Scriptures is Psalm 37:4: "Take delight in the LORD, and he will give you the desires of your heart." Some people take that to mean that he will give you the things that you desire. I take it to mean that he will *plant within you* the desires he designed you to have. As we delight in him, he shapes the desires of our hearts, the very desires and dreams that he put there—that he sang there—in the first place.

Discovering Your Voice

God created you and delights in you. He gifted you. Consider how God's voice has called to you through your natural giftedness.

- What desires has God planted in your heart?
- If you think of your God-given gifts and interests as your language, what language do you speak?
- What language does God speak to you? For me, it is the language of music. For some, it is the language of nature or poetry or creativity or art or science.

Meditate on Psalm 29:4, asking yourself, "How do I hear the voice of God most clearly?"

> The **voice** of the LORD is powerful;
> the **voice** of the LORD is majestic.

At the end of each chapter of this book is a Bible verse that uses the word *voice* so that we can explore what God's Word has to say about it. I have printed **voice** in boldface each time to help us read the verse with a fresh perspective.

CHAPTER TWO

Resetting the Clock

One day in some hotel in some city on some tour, I looked at the clock by the bedside and noticed I had two whole hours until I had to leave for the airport. Ahh. A lovely lazy morning in my hotel room. I lounged in bed, caught up on social media, nabbed a pair of shoes online that I was going to need in December (50 percent off, thank you very much), and took my time. When I began to pack, I looked at the time on my phone and with a thud in my heart understood that the clock in the room was wrong! I had based all my plans and relaxed feelings on what I thought was the truth, only to find out it was not the truth at all.

The sudden realization that I had an extremely short time to get ready sent me into a tailspin. The revelation of the actual time brought chaos and turmoil, but it was true, and I had to adjust my distorted reality to that truth. The truth cost me in that moment. It cost me my happy attitude. It cost me a shower. It cost me a neatly packed suitcase and a well-groomed appearance, but in the end, the false truth would have cost me way more.

While I was on my way to the airport with my disheveled self, it dawned on me that I had spent most of my early adult years deliciously ignorant of the truth in my life. And when I found it, it sent me into a tailspin for a while. But oh my. Now I sit with joy and satisfaction right smack dab in the middle of the truth that more often than not doesn't look pretty. But I've learned not to run from it. Now I just wait with confidence, knowing that it is far better to wait in the truth than to live in a lie.

I must tell you that this chapter is very hard for me to write. I'd rather sing you a song, but too many words need to be said, and they won't all fit poetically into a melody. So, this is me . . . writing. It's a hard topic to tackle, but here we go. Because we need to talk about it.

Sexual abuse.

Let those two words sit there for just a second. The story behind them redirected my view of life. It redirected how I saw the world around me and how I interpreted the things going on inside me. Those two words set my clock *wrong*. Terribly wrong. And it has taken me years to reset the inner workings of my world to what is true.

Vulnerable

I was six years old. I was a compliant and good-natured kid with slightly curly reddish-blonde hair and blue-green eyes. My dad's choir at our Arizona church was honestly amazing. The church, my dad, and the choir were so good, they had a television show every Sunday afternoon. These were fun years filled with much music. Because my parents were the music and worship leaders, I was at church about eight days a week.

My parents also had a quartet they traveled with once or twice a year. My mom was the pianist and Dad was one of the voices. Now that I was a big first grader, the arrangements for their travel were different than in past years. It used to be that when my parents traveled, someone would stay with my brothers and me at the house. But because this year I was in school, they felt it was important that I stay with someone who could be a bridge for me with school. She was a friend of my parents, and she was also a first-grade schoolteacher. Although she taught at a different school, the plan was for me to accompany her to her class so I wouldn't fall behind in my schoolwork. (I needed to keep up with my reading!)

Arrangements were made, and I was set to stay with this woman. Let's call her Helen. My parents assumed she lived alone. But her mother lived with her. To be honest, the moment I walked into Helen's house and saw her mom, I was uncomfortable. I didn't have words for this discomfort. I still don't. I just sensed a wrongness in the place.

I liked Helen well enough when I saw her in other settings. And I know that my parents wouldn't have arranged for me to stay with her if they hadn't felt comfortable and trusted her. But the minute my parents dropped me off and we said goodbye, Helen changed. Her face changed from sweet to hard, her manner from kind to stern, even angry. The house changed, too. I can't explain it except to say that it totally creeped me out.

Let me put a couple of things in context here. This was 1962. There were no cell phones, no email, no pagers, no answering machines. No nothing. Just a landline phone at the house. I'm certain that my parents had Helen's house phone number. And I know my mom well enough that I know she would have written out all the names of the churches where they were performing, along with the phone numbers, as well as any motels where they would be staying. But in my mind, as a six-year-old girl, there didn't seem to be a way I could communicate with my parents. They called to check in on me, but I remember them talking only to Helen. I don't remember Helen ever saying to me, "Would you like to say hi to your parents?"

A six-year-old doesn't really have a lot of words anyway—especially me! I certainly didn't know how to speak up or even dare to ask to call my parents. There was this "don't misbehave or else" feeling. So, being a good-natured, compliant kid, I behaved. Believe me, I behaved!

As it got near bedtime the first night, a plate of chocolate chip cookies appeared on the counter. I *loved* chocolate chip cookies. They were my favorite, and I remember thinking, *Okay, this is better. I can like this.* I ate a few—with some milk. (Still the best snack ever.)

Then Helen said, "It's time to get ready for bed. Go get your pajamas on." I went into the room where I would be staying for the week and realized there were two beds. This was also Helen's room. Hmm. I squirmed at the thought, though I wasn't sure why. I remember going into the bathroom that was attached to the bedroom, because that's where my suitcase was. As I scrounged through my things, I couldn't find my favorite nightgown. You know, the one that's all tattered and torn and is the most comfortable thing ever? I finally spied it on the bottom of my suitcase and put it on, brushed my teeth, and headed to bed.

Helen came in and said, "Why do you have that ugly thing on? Here." She tossed me a beautiful, brand-new, white nightgown. "Wear this." And instead of saying, "But this is my favorite," compliant, voiceless me quietly discarded my favorite gown for the new one, thinking perhaps my mom had surprised me and put that new gown in my suitcase.

As odd as it was to share a room with an adult, I managed to slip deeply into sleep. I woke up in the middle of the night to a very strange sensation. As I lay there, pretending to still be asleep, I took inventory of my surroundings. Yes, I was still in the bed. Yes, I was still at Helen's house. Wait. Where was my nightgown? Had someone removed it? I was lying facedown on the bed, devoid of clothes. This made no sense. Trying to clue in to what else was happening, I realized that Helen was "washing" my private female area. I remember thinking, *Do not let her know you are awake. Just lie here and don't move.* Something in me told me that it could be worse if I suddenly "woke up." All I could think to do was just "behave." So I stayed still for a very, very long time as the touching continued.

Helen finally finished whatever it was she was doing to me. I listened intently to find out what would happen next. After going to the bathroom, she slipped back into her bed. Still, I waited. I waited until I heard her breathing evenly, in and out, until I knew (at least really hoped) she was asleep. Then I quietly got up from my bed and went into the bathroom to my suitcase and looked for the nightgown that I had had on when I went to bed—the new one—but I couldn't find it. Determined not to sleep gownless, I grabbed my favorite and put that back on and hurried to bed.

The next morning as we woke up and began to get ready to go to school, she saw that I had my favorite gown on and said, "I told you not to wear that ugly one. Why did you put it back on?"

Seriously? I couldn't believe she even asked. I wanted to say, *Because, you idiot, you took my gown off me and did stuff to me while I was lying gownless on the bed.* At least that's what I said in

29

my head. But I never said it out loud to her. Or to anyone else, until decades later.

The next day, as evening approached, I felt myself getting anxious and wishing so much that I could call my parents to come and get me. All I could do was hope that the same things wouldn't happen again. And then the cookies and milk appeared.

This same nighttime routine continued every single night that I stayed at Helen's house. Cookies and milk. Favorite nightgown. Nope—put the new one on. Waking up in the middle of the night lying facedown on the bed. Helen doing things. Going back to sleep. Can't find the new gown, put the favorite back on. *Every single night.* It became "normal," and I just came to expect it. Somehow, I managed to continue to pretend to sleep through the horrible, confusing nightmare. I hated it but felt utterly voiceless and powerless, so I kept my eyes closed and somehow shut down my emotions.

During the day, we went to the school where Helen was the first-grade teacher. I went with her to class. I was a good kid. I was shy and complied and behaved. I was just a visitor to this school, so the very last thing I ever would have wanted to do was misbehave. I was already really embarrassed by being the "new" kid, yet I was quietly making friends. One day, midweek, the students were working in groups of three or four, cutting out pictures and pasting them. All of a sudden, Helen said loudly, "Sandy, go stand in the corner." I froze, dumbfounded. Again, she said, "Sandy, I said go stand in the corner. You're in trouble." I can honestly say I had done nothing wrong, especially since I was trying very hard not to be seen.

Embarrassed and humiliated, I got up from the table and went to stand in the corner with no idea what I had done. Helen gave no explanation. Giggling from some of the kids devastated me. I don't even know how long I stayed there, but after a time, Helen said, "Go sit down." Still no explanation. Nothing.

You know what is so bizarre? I remember thinking the whole time, *Please don't tell my parents. I'll be in even bigger trouble.* Somehow I had assumed the blame, but for what I didn't even know. And then I began to think, *Well, maybe it's my fault, too, that Helen comes to me in the middle of the night. It's because I am a bad girl. I am to blame.*

I assumed my conclusions were right because adults don't hurt children. Adults don't humiliate children. Adults are safe. Therefore, *I* must be the one to blame. *I* am the one at fault. That was reinforced the day before my parents were to return home when Helen told me, a mean look on her face, "If you tell your parents what happened while you were here, they won't believe you. And I'll come find you and do this to you again."

And just like that—in one short week that seemed to last forever—my clock was reset. It was reset so it no longer accurately reflected truth. It was wrong.

Never Enough

Here's a sidebar that I simply must share with you. I told you this would be a hard chapter to write. It has been more than hard. Even as I've been typing it I've needed to stop and walk around the kitchen praying and talking to God loudly. I also called some dear friends asking them to cover me with prayer because I felt so many horrible feelings—including fear. God in his awesomeness reminded me quietly of two things. One, he did not send the spirit of fear, so the fear I was feeling? Totally not from God. God sends power, love, and a sound mind, as revealed in 2 Timothy 1:7 (NKJV). God nudged that little verse to the forefront of my mind, and I claimed it. And second, I am loved. My dear hubby—my sweet prayer partner, life mate, best friend—just showed up at the house with my favorite Starbucks drink, just because. Now, you can't tell me God doesn't see us.

So from the age of six, I walked through my unconscious life looking through the lens of always being the bad girl and everything being my fault. And I did so because I believed that a lie was the truth. It played out in every area of my life except music. I was never (in my view) smart enough or thin enough or fast enough or nice enough or pretty enough. As I viewed life through the lie, I could see that the very core of me was never enough. And when your core is lacking, your voice is afraid to express itself and is nearly snuffed out. Silencing your voice is the only way to make certain you can hide behind a mask of being whoever you want others to think you are.

I walked through life seeing myself as damaged goods—what a terrible weight to bear! But the clock must be right, right? All I wanted to do was hide. Along with silencing my voice, I found a great hiding place with food. Because the more food you eat, the more layers you have and the more insulation you build up so no one can get to you. Of course, you can't get to anyone else either.

Many years passed before I understood just how badly my clock had been set, and how to really listen to and lean into God's Word of truth. Until then, I moved through life with my *being* based on a clock *that was wrong*.

I am so thankful that God wasn't content to leave me with my clock set wrong. He put a plan in place to reset it. Looking back, I can see that clearly.

Discovering Your Voice

Oh, child of God, you are so madly and passionately loved by the God of this universe. You are his creation, and he doesn't make mistakes. He knows your name. He sees you. You are not a person unworthy of his love—no matter what you have done or what has been done to you. He delights in *you*. He chooses you. He chooses me. This is just simply true. So ask yourself:

- What event(s) in your life set your clock wrong?
- How did that affect your voice?
- Are you willing to do whatever it takes to reset your clock to the truth? What is the first step you need to take?

I cannot emphasize enough the value Christian counseling has added to my life. The deep, murky waters of child abuse or other deep wounds we carry cannot be navigated alone. It is hard and exhausting and the journey will feel meaningless at times, but I promise you it is worth it. I also promise you that you are not alone. If you are beginning this journey, whether because of some abuse in your past or some other deep wound, press in and press on! *You* are so worth it.

Listen to the psalmist's voice in Psalm 18:6:

> In my distress I called to the Lord;
> I cried to my God for help.
> From his temple he heard my **voice**;
> my cry came before him, into his ears.

CHAPTER THREE

Who Said I Shouldn't Talk?

Recently my son-in-law Collin had a suspicious irregular area on his skin that the doctor needed to remove. It just so happened to be on his upper left chest, where you put your hand over your heart when you say the Pledge of Allegiance. Thankfully, it was benign. Not long afterward, I was Facetiming with my grandson, Thatcher, Collin's four-year-old son.

"Nani, my dad had to have a piece of his heart taken out," Thatcher explained to me, "but the doctor put his heart back together and he got to get stitches."

His interpretation of the event was adorable and has already become part of the fabric of fun family storytelling, but it illustrates how children can misinterpret the messages they receive. Of course, Thatcher's mom and dad hadn't wanted to say, "Hey, pal, Daddy might have skin cancer, which is really terrible, and we just want to make sure that the doctor gets all the suspicious cells." They had simply explained, "Daddy has an owie and the doctor needs to fix it." But Thatcher put two and two together from his four-year-old perspective and concluded that the doctor had to take out a piece of his daddy's heart. Fortunately, once Thatcher's parents discovered his misconception, they were able to help him understand the difference between Daddy's heart and the skin on Daddy's chest.

Let's face it. Kids filter what they see and hear through their limited view of the world. They assume many things that make sense to them but are far from reality.

I got the message early on that my voice—sharing my thoughts and feelings—didn't matter. At least that's how I put together the messages I was receiving. As with Thatcher, however, my conclusions were certainly not what my parents intended. Sadly, they never knew the message I was assuming, and so they could not set the record straight.

And remember, my clock was set wrong by the sexual abuse I experienced at the tender age of six, so I wasn't interpreting correctly much of the information I was processing. My abuser had said, "Don't you tell anyone. They won't believe you anyway. And it's your fault." I walked away from that sexual abuse with the understanding that I was a bad girl who had brought bad things upon herself. Too afraid to tell anyone, too traumatized and innocent to process correctly what had happened to me, I kept that secret locked away deep inside, where it festered, poisoning my image of myself and reinforcing the idea that bad things inside of me should stay locked away in the dark where no one could see them.

And then there was the fact that I was an introvert. Shy by nature, I found it difficult to fit into the world of relationships around me. Added to the trauma, my introversion reinforced the distorted lens through which I viewed self-expression.

I've done some research on personality types and discovered that my personality type highly values harmony and despises conflict. I like to please others, and I find conflict extremely disagreeable—something to be avoided at all costs. Add these factors together and you have the setup for a little girl who kept negative thoughts and feelings stuffed down in the dark depths within. Many years later, in counseling, I realized that I was six when I started to believe the message that my words didn't matter.

I'm sure no one ever actually said to me, "Your feelings don't matter, so hush." My parents certainly didn't tell me that my voice didn't matter. But they also didn't teach me *how* to use that voice. My parents' generation didn't talk about feelings all that much. As I have listened to them over the years, I've come to realize that their childhood was hard. They were children during World War II. The fear that Germany might win the war dominated their childhood and far outweighed personal matters. Their parents worried about where the next meal would come from and how to pay for necessities such as new school supplies. When beans and cornbread were served for dinner night after night, they were thankful not to go hungry. Because these were the kinds of issues that occupied their thoughts as children, I find no fault with my mom and dad for not really fostering an environment for communication when they became parents.

It didn't help that I never heard my parents argue or fuss or disagree. Seriously! (Years later I learned that they did argue, but only in private.) Consequently, I never saw conflict resolution modeled. I simply assumed that people who love each other don't argue. I also somehow assumed, *Don't speak up or you will be the cause of conflict.*

Another factor contributing to my silent voice was my interpretation that the church taught that anger is a sin. Of course, later I learned that anger is not a sin, that even God gets angry. It is what we choose to *do* with our anger that can become sinful. But such subtleties were lost on me as a child. So, as I was growing up, my conclusions were, *Don't make waves. If you have a feeling that seems uncomfortable or negative, don't say it, because then you will cause conflict.* These weren't the messages my church or parents intended to teach me, but they were my takeaway.

So my voice, my opinions, my thoughts, my feelings didn't seem to matter. Nevertheless, those opinions, thoughts, and feelings were in me. I just didn't know how to get them out. And guess what? Food helped me keep those things silenced and packed down. Anytime I thought about saying something or sharing my opinion, food conveniently was available to take the place of words. It took the edge off for a bit. But turning to food also resulted in my associating it with bad thoughts about myself. Because the horrifying routine of the abuse began with my eating chocolate chip cookies as a bedtime snack, I connected feelings of discomfort with the desire to eat chocolate chip cookies.

Yet chocolate chip cookies are so delicious and desirable. (And let's be real here—chocolate solves so many problems!) And so are a lot of other things—movie popcorn, ice cream, extra helpings of anything. For a nanosecond, food quiets the demons and soothes the voices. The problem, of course, is the calories they bring. The more I had to say, the more I ate to bury it, and the more my body grew. A horrific cycle began, one that in years to come kept me stuck in the spin cycle. I piled layer upon layer, literally and figuratively, that left me feeling separated and disconnected from others.

Silenced

I remember two times when I tried to speak up and stand up for myself, both ending in what, for me, were disastrous consequences.

One day when I was in sixth or seventh grade, I was walking home from a softball game with a friend of mine. She grabbed my softball mitt and started what I thought was just a game of keep-away. "Hey, give it back," I called out playfully as I chased her for a bit and grabbed my mitt back along with hers. As I ran, she chased me, but when she caught up to me, instead of laughing and retrieving her mitt, she hit me so hard in the back that it knocked the wind out of me and I fell to the ground. I was coughing and couldn't catch my breath, which frightened me. I started crying, but to save face I pretended I was laughing. I grabbed my mitt and said something about needing to get home. I cried all the way home and prayed that my mom or dad would just happen to drive by, because I didn't think I was going to make it. I felt so stupid. (I have never been a good "player" or "have fun" person, and I've never taken teasing well at all.) I cried, thinking, *See, if you had just kept quiet and not tried to speak up in order to get your mitt back, none of this would have happened.*

When I finally got home, my parents immediately knew something was wrong. Now, because my parents' intent was to help me always defer to and serve others, I often got the message that conflict was my fault, so when faced with it, I rarely told my parents. I feared it would just circle back to the fact that I caused it, which I usually believed anyway. I was already prone to take the blame. But this time, I told them what had happened, feeling quite justified to be upset. Then my sweet dad, who meant well, said, "Sandy, what did you do to cause her to hit you?"

Really? I thought. *He just assumes this is my fault?*

"Dad, she *hit* me!"

"But why?"

"Because I stole her mitt, but she stole mine first. And we were just playing and goofing around." Dad just looked at me as if waiting for me to realize how wrong I'd been. I thought, *Don't you get it? She hit me so hard I couldn't even breathe.* I wanted to say, "Dad, I need you to be on my side here," but I couldn't voice those words.

God love him, he said, "Well, maybe you need to be the first to apologize." Again, inside I cried, *Are you kidding me?* I was so mad, but I had learned (and clearly this new lesson underlined the fact) that my voice did not matter. My inner voice shouted, *I didn't do anything wrong! Why do I need to apologize?* but not a sound came out. I felt I had only two options: be seen as an ogre and be angry, or take the blame, be the "bigger" (pun intended) person, and apologize. I did apologize, like a good little Christian girl, but it left me feeling victimized and silenced. And I continued to become the "bigger" person . . . literally.

The other incident happened when I was in eighth grade. I had a friend who was so cool I thought she was doing me a favor by being my friend. We hung out at lunch, played volleyball together, and walked part of the way home together. One day when we were walking home, I accidently stepped on the back of her heel and her shoe came off. I just wasn't paying attention. It was an accident, and I felt terrible because, remember, I never ever wanted to do anything to make other people uncomfortable.

She stomped away, furious, and didn't talk to me for an entire week. I wept every night privately in my bed. Even now as I write, a grown woman decades later, I remember my grief so well it hurts.

Having a friendship like hers meant so much to me, an introverted, lonely adolescent girl. I tried so hard to be a good friend, and now I'd lost her over something unintended.

As the week went on and the silent treatment continued, I even wrote her a note to tell her I was sorry and sent it through a mutual friend at school. She sent it back having never even read it. Once again, my voice had been shut down. It didn't matter.

This time, however, my mom's response soothed my pain. I cried so much at home that my sweet mom came in my room and said, "Honey, what's the matter? What happened?" I told her what had happened, that I hadn't meant to hurt my friend, and that it had been a total accident. I ended with, "And now she won't even talk to me."

I will never forget my mom's compassion. There on my bed, she scooped me up in her arms and just held me, saying, "Honey, I'm so sorry. I think your friend will come around, but I'm so, so sorry." Mom's words didn't fix it or make it all go away, but I felt like she heard and welcomed my voice of pain and hurt.

As you can see, in both instances, I felt so relationally inept that when I encountered conflict, I didn't know what to do about it. Without having conflict resolution modeled for me, I assumed all the fault was mine. I lacked the skills to bounce back and resolve it on my own. Fairly minor incidents that many kids would have brushed off or worked through left me so devastated that even now they have the power to bring tears to my eyes. In such incidents, I believed that if I could just be sensitive enough or kind enough or skinny enough or good enough, I could head off all these conflicts. They wouldn't happen if only I could do better. So I tried all the harder to do and be better.

Learning to Talk

My experience demonstrates how important it is to create an environment to teach kids how to express their thoughts and feelings. Just because a child is shy doesn't mean she doesn't have something to say. One thing that Don and I tried to do when our kids were little was to set an atmosphere where we could all learn how to talk to each other. At family dinners, we began a tradition of going around the table and telling each other our high of the day and our low of the day. We intentionally modeled four things: that everyone has something to say, that everyone gets a turn to communicate, that it's okay to have something in the day you didn't like, and that it's okay to express that something you didn't like. I believe I was desperately trying to break the cycle of noncommunication.

When the kids were little, the highs covered such things as, "We had an extra-long recess today."

"Yay!" everyone would say.

A low might be, "We had a substitute today, and she wasn't nice."

"Oh, that's hard, dude. So sorry." Just acknowledging that all those feelings were okay and that our children had every right to voice them accomplished our goals. As the kids got older, the highs and the lows became more meaningful.

"This kid called me ugly."

"So-and-so asked me to the prom."

"Mom, I told you I would come right home, but I lied to you."

If we don't initiate and welcome conversation and foster a safe environment for it, conversation will not happen, and if we don't do so when our kids are young, it certainly won't magically begin when they become teenagers. Don and I very much wanted to create a home where the kids could say anything and know they were safe. And believe me, we heard a lot of things. Sometimes I wanted to put my fingers in my ears and just go, "La la la la." But I stayed in the conversation because I desperately wanted them to know that their voices matter.

Now, I'm not going to tell you that every time the kids came to us we responded with, "Yes, honey, I hear you." There were times we said, "I'm sorry, *what*? You did *what*? Are you out of your mind?" That's when we as parents needed a timeout! Sometimes, I confess, I was tempted to say, "Okay, your voice doesn't matter *that* much. You can stop now." Yet I believe, seeing how well they all communicate now as adults, that they got the message. And that makes me happy. It feels healing for me because I think it redeems the pain I suffered before I found my voice.

Preparation

Because I wasn't raised in an environment that fostered the use of my speaking voice, I am grateful for the language of music that my parents lavished upon me. When words failed me, music was always my outlet.

One part of my musical voice was the piano. My mother insisted that my two brothers and I learn how to play. When I was younger, I hated having to practice every day after school, but as I became proficient, I could pound out my frustrations or soothe them away in that rich musical language that seems able to touch every emotion. Learning to understand and play the piano became the foundation of my musical, as well as emotional, education.

The Voice

When I was in the eighth grade, we moved from Phoenix to San Diego. Here I learned of the various choirs available to me when I reached high school, and I couldn't wait. At the end of the year, I auditioned for the madrigals, the high school choir I dreamed of belonging to. My proficiency in piano along with the many musical experiences my parents provided at home and at church, and the superb coaching of my beloved elementary music teacher, all contributed to my readiness for this elite choir. I made the cut and eagerly anticipated my high school adventure.

Discovering Your Voice

You can explore your past to gain a clearer perspective on the factors that influenced the development of your voice. This may give you insight into how best to release your voice today. Consider these questions:

- What experiences in your childhood hindered your voice— the ability to express your thoughts and feelings?
- What experience, person, or activity enabled you to give voice to your deepest longings?
- What might help you to release your voice today?

For some, reading is their avenue of exploring, experiencing, and finding words for their thoughts and feelings. For others, athletics or art or acts of service give them the means to self-express. Though my voice went largely unused in my childhood, the language of music tapped into my soul and offered me the self-expression I desperately needed. It also ushered me into a spirit of prayer and worship that became part of the fabric of my life. This verse, found in 2 Chronicles 5:13, speaks my heart:

> The trumpeters and musicians joined in unison to give praise and thanks to the Lord. Accompanied by trumpets, cymbals and other instruments, the singers raised their **voices** in praise to the Lord and sang: "He is good; his love endures forever."

CHAPTER FOUR

Unfiltered

I dove into my high school years headfirst and in a hurry. Not an elegant, graceful dive, mind you. More of a belly flop. You know, the kind of dive that lands with the sound of a loud slap (instead of a smooth swoosh), drenches all the onlookers with an unpleasant splash, and makes you look like a fool. I don't like to talk about high school much because to tell you the truth, I don't understand the high school me at all. She feels much like I think Peter Pan's shadow might feel to him—it's there and it's supposed to be a part of you, but it has a mind of its own and is very annoying.

To put it simply, the teenage Sandi embarrasses me to this day. It's as if the once-voiceless child changed overnight into a high school teenager who was determined to speak out, but who said all the wrong things. Well, not *all* the wrong things—there were some shining moments.

Madrigals began as a shining moment. To enter high school as a freshman already a member of the most prestigious musical group at the school was a huge boost to my fragile self-image. I was even asked to play piano for some rehearsals, which increased that positive effect. (Thanks, Mom, for making me take those lessons!) Walking into the choir room was the highlight of each day. Take the challenge of the music, the quality of the group's performances, the pure joy of letting my voice ring out in harmony with others, and add them to the intense emotions of a ninth-grade girl, and you have an explosive "it doesn't get better than this" experience. My voice was given wings to fly, and it soared. What a rush!

But it got even better! In 1970 and 1971 (my freshman and sophomore years), our choir attended several workshops to learn about the transition from a traditional choir to the show choir that a number of schools were doing. This new trend took the choir from standing still and singing a cappella (which was already awesome) to doing choreography. The girls even switched to shorter skirts and go-go boots. We were the bomb!

But then it got complicated.

Clueless

In my sophomore year, my teacher asked me if I had any ideas on what we should do to better our program. It was like saying "sic 'em" to a dog. I was pumped. This was my language! My mind started racing not only with musical arrangements but also with choreographic ideas. I had never been a dancer but had always wanted to be, so this was a fun and exciting challenge. But it became far more than that for me. Let's just say I got a little carried away asserting my opinions. (New territory for me.) My teacher had asked me for ideas, not to take over. But I was young and immature and I didn't know healthy boundaries. So I dove in. *Splat.*

I "suggested" lots of things for that program. Afterward, I kept right on suggesting more. For example, I created a medley of songs from the 1920s to the present. I took it to class one day and announced to my choir teacher, "I have a medley I'd like to teach the class," and she let me.

For the next few weeks, the class worked on this medley under my direction. It honestly was pretty good, and the kids really loved it.

But because such boldness was highly uncharacteristic of me, I didn't realize I was being bossy and overbearing. No one had ever mentioned before that I was bossy. (Well, except for my brothers, but they didn't count to a big sister.) I thought I was simply helping the teacher. I guess when you have no boundaries, that's how you might see yourself. As I look back, the teacher could have said, "Dear, I'm the teacher and you are the student." Maybe that would have clued me in to the fact that she felt I was overstepping my bounds. If she did send such clues, they went right over my head. I simply did not see or hear them.

After two years of enduring my pushiness, my teacher gave me a B on my junior year report card. I was shocked. Clearly she didn't realize how much I'd done for the class! (My perspective, not hers.) I scheduled an appointment with her to ask why I'd been given a B. She hemmed and hawed and said something about a couple of my higher notes being flat or something like that. I honestly was so hurt and offended that I decided to quit madrigals at the end of the year.

I should qualify that. I had two incentives to quit music. The end of junior year is the time to try out for a variety of senior year activities. I wanted to try out for two of my other high school dreams—to be a cheerleader and to be in the school musical. Our school had a rather bizarre practice—the music department and the drama department did not work together at all. If a student wanted to take drama and be in the musical, they couldn't take music as well. (How odd is that?) When my advisor saw that I was quitting music, she called me in to her office. "For heaven's sake," she said, "why are you quitting music?"

(Get ready to cringe!) I told her quite simply, "I think the teacher is jealous of me and all of the ways I helped her teach the class." Can you imagine the audacity of this talented, yet completely clueless, younger me? My voice was now in full force, yet sadly lacked appropriate filters!

Then I told my counselor that I really wanted to do the musical, and I couldn't be in drama and choir at the same time. She nodded and said, "Okay, then. It's your decision."

I auditioned for both drama class and cheerleading. Within a few days, the drama teacher called me down for a private meeting in the auditorium. I had no idea why and was nervous.

"I've heard some things that other teachers have said about you. In particular, the music teacher," he said. My stomach lurched. *What is happening?* my inner voice cried out.

"She told me that I should not let you into the drama class because you take over and don't listen to the teacher or respect authority."

Seriously? I thought. *I basically saved her. She can't sing. She can't play the piano. She can't lead.*

Ugh. Teenage Sandi, unfiltered. Yes, the arrogance is evident, and so, too, the hurt I felt. I had no idea how to resolve conflict. I had no idea how to see myself through other people's eyes. I just assumed that my ideas were the best and that was that.

I said to the drama teacher, "It was not my intention to take over. I really thought she was welcoming my help." Suddenly the B on my report card made sense. I did a quick flashback over the previous couple of years and realized that my music teacher had never asked me or given me permission to take over. I just did because I thought I knew what was best for the group. I had simply asserted myself. Now I recoiled at the consequences and decided not to make that mistake again.

In retrospect, of course, I see that the music teacher evidently didn't know how to confront me and have a conversation about her expectations. Perhaps her own voice wasn't strong and confident.

As I spoke with the drama teacher, he heard my heart rather than just what he had heard about me. He told me he would be happy to have me in the drama class, which, to this day, I greatly appreciate.

To my surprise and delight, I also made it onto the cheerleading squad. Let me just say there was nothing physical about me that made me believe I'd be chosen as a cheerleader. I was always referred to as "thick" or "chubby." But I was enthusiastic. And I could yell. Loud! And I'm pretty sure that's what helped me get onto the squad. I couldn't tumble. I couldn't jump very high. But I had a lot of spirit and strong vocal cords. So they picked me. I was elated! We spent all summer practicing and went to cheer camp. I had an awesome summer and headed into my senior year on an incredibly positive note. A swoosh rather than a splat.

Invited to Lead

As the new school year began, I took my place as one of about sixteen girls on the cheerleading squad. We were divided into two groups—the cheerleaders, whose job it was to chant and fire up the crowd, and the song leaders, who looked beautiful and danced and did all the tumbling. (They were awesome.) There was a head cheerleader and a head song leader—neither of which I was chosen for, even though I *knew* I had better ideas than anyone. (Yes, the immaturity and arrogance were still there. I just kept my thoughts to myself this time. I'm glad people couldn't peek into my head and see them. Inside, I was not a very nice person. I'm not sure I would have wanted to be my own friend.)

One of the responsibilities of the cheer squad was to plan the pep rallies before football and basketball games. We would get together after school to plan, but no one seemed to have any good ideas. I kept quiet on purpose, thinking I didn't want to repeat what had happened in madrigals and have anyone thinking I was taking over. I really was trying to learn from my mistakes.

One day everyone started bickering about ideas for the upcoming pep rally. Oh my—so much emotion in a group of adolescent girls! Finally someone said to me, "Sandi, what do you think? You haven't said anything."

I caught my breath and said, "Well, I didn't want to get in the way of the captains."

One of the girls said, "Seriously, let's face it. Sandi always has the best ideas. Let's listen to her."

The group chimed in, "Yeah, please help us." Their words were gratifying to hear.

All my life I had watched my dad put services and concerts together, so I felt like I understood something about designing the flow for an event. This time, I knew I was leading at the request of the group, so I became the one who basically produced the pep rallies, asking the coach to say something here and there and asking a couple of the guys on the team to help us with a skit here and there.

I really loved that kind of thing (and still do). And though my body shape never changed, I loved that time as a cheerleader in high school.

Meanwhile, the drama teacher announced that we would be performing *West Side Story* for the year's musical.

Are you kidding me? I thought. *I love that musical!* I had seen the movie with Natalie Wood and adored the music. I felt I could sing her part, but I definitely didn't look like the leading lady for *West Side Story*. After all, I was the thick one. And I definitely wasn't Puerto Rican. I was blonde, blue-eyed, and anything but petite. But I wanted so much to play that part and sing those beautiful songs.

Fortunately, being so active in cheerleading had helped me look not quite so thick. With a little self-tanner (which looked awfully unnatural in the seventies) and a dark hair rinse, I could look a little bit more like the leading lady.

The day came for the audition. I had chosen to sing "Somewhere" from the musical. I began with those promising words, "There's a place for us" (hoping against hope there would be a place for me!). Judging by the teacher's response, I did well. After the auditions were over, he told the class that he couldn't decide who should play Maria. He'd narrowed it down to two of us. (A little note to teachers: don't ever tell your class something like that.) Instead of deciding himself, he had the entire class vote. How agonizing that was for me! The other contender was lovely and sang beautifully. She had long dark hair and really looked the part. However, to my absolute delight, my class voted for me to play Maria.

Everything about the experience of that musical was a dream come true. I loved preparing for the role—working on my Puerto Rican accent and learning the songs that were so moving and beautiful. Each time I took the stage singing that there was a "time for us" and a "place for us," my heart swelled with the feeling that *I* was in that time and place. I'd stepped into my *voice,* right there, in the spotlight. To this day that show is still one of the highlights of my life. That experience inspired me to entertain the idea of going to UCLA to study musical theater.

Fun fact: One of the other students in my drama class was Kathy Najimy. She went on to be a wonderful actress in Los Angeles and is probably known best for her roles in *Sister Act* and *Hocus Pocus.*

On a Low Note

Of course, no discussion of high school would be complete without talking about boyfriends. Paradoxically, though my confidence soared when I took the stage or produced the cheerleader events, offstage I was the least confident person I knew. I saw myself as fat and ugly. So interaction with boys was completely awkward and weird for me. I didn't know how to act with them.

Around boys I didn't feel romantically interested in, I acted casual and friendly. However, at times this led them to believe that I liked them, which resulted in their having a crush on me. I never once saw this coming. Before I knew it, one of them would ask me for a date. *Hmmm. Okay. Maybe this is cool,* I'd think. So I'd end up dating someone I honestly wasn't attracted to, thinking that since I was unattractive, this was probably the best it would get for me. Conversely, if I was interested in a boy, I froze up and became invisible. I just couldn't seem to catch on to the language of boys.

In my senior year, I went out for a time with a young man from church who seemed to genuinely love me. For a little while, I thought

I loved him, too. But eventually I broke it off, believing you had to find your true love in college. My high school self was so weird!

At the end of the school year, a boy who was a friend asked me to go to the prom. I agreed. As prom night approached, however—oh my, this isn't going to be a pretty story! As the prom approached, a boy I'd been friends with all through high school (I'll call him Jay) broke up with his girlfriend, and he and I realized we liked each other. But we each had a date with someone else for the prom.

The prom tradition at our school was to hang out after the prom, and then the next day, though exhausted, we'd all get on a bus and go to Disneyland together.

During my prom, I hate to confess, Jay and I each ditched our dates and hung out with each other. As if that wasn't bad enough, we then did something really horrible. We agreed that before we got on the bus the next day, we'd call our dates and tell them we were going to Disneyland not with them but with each other. I know—so disrespectful and insensitive.

As the day at Disneyland wore on, though, I began to feel horrible. I knew what I had done was utterly wrong. So I determined that when I got home, I was going to go to the two wronged people and apologize. I had no idea whether they would accept my apology, but I knew that was what I had to do. The Disneyland bus didn't get us back home until very late Saturday night. The only thing I knew to do was to show up at their houses sometime on Sunday.

I called each of them ahead of time and said, "May I please come over and talk to you in person? I'm sure I'm the last person you want to see right now, but may I please?" They both said yes, so I went and, one at a time, knocked on their respective doors. I trembled, waiting for them to appear in the doorway. When they did, I said,

"I want you to know that I understand what I did to you was wrong. And you have no reason to forgive me. But I would like to say that I am sorry, and I ask you to forgive me."

The conversations didn't take very long because they pretty much said, "I'm not sure I can do that right now."

I said, "I understand, but I still had to come and tell you that in person." Both of them then shut the door. But it didn't end there, because I took that guilt and shame back home with me. I nursed it and carried it, and it left a huge self-imposed scar on me.

For years I told myself that I never went to homecoming or class reunions because I didn't want to be remembered as the thick cheerleader. But the absolute truth is I didn't go back because I was so deeply embarrassed at my behavior that weekend. I had used my voice to hurt two people deeply.

Even today, I have a hard time reconciling that younger self with my older self. I don't like that younger me. That last act of high school leaves me believing she was just selfish. But "she" is "me." And if I cannot accept her, which in many ways was the worst of me, then how can I really take in and appreciate God's grace?

It took me many years to learn that I had only one healthy choice for dealing with that shame. I must use my voice to confess my selfishness, then take it to Jesus and leave it there at the foot of the cross, knowing that in his act of loving sacrifice, he forgave it all.

When I Was a Child

First Corinthians 13 is known as "the love chapter." It defines love as being patient and kind and explains that it does not dishonor others and is not self-seeking. Unquestionably, I did not act out of love on prom night. But it goes on to say in verse 11, "When I was a child, I talked like a child, I thought like a child, I reasoned like a child. When I became a man, I put the ways of childhood behind me."

Yes, as immature people we may use our voices in harmful ways, but as we mature, we can put those childish ways behind us. I love verse 12: "For now we see only a reflection as in a mirror; then we shall see face to face. Now I know in part; then I shall know fully, even as I am fully known."

You and I are fully known and fully loved. Verse 5 tells us that love keeps no record of wrongs. Isn't that awesome? God is not keeping a record of our wrongs, for he has covered them with his love.

Today, I strive to use my high school years as a reminder that childhood and adolescence are preparation for adulthood, and that includes our mistakes as well as our good choices. I see that during those years, God gave me rich opportunities to step into my voice. At times, I used those moments well and exercised my voice with creativity. At times, I misused my voice and became overbearing or bossy or downright cruel. The important thing today is to learn from those experiences—to take "voice lessons" and to make wise choices today and tomorrow.

Discovering Your Voice

No matter the choices we have made in the past, *today* offers a new opportunity to make God-honoring choices and grow from our experiences. As you look back on your life, ask yourself:

- What experiences did God provide for you that opened new doors to use your voice?
- Which of those experiences did you use unwisely? Have you been able to forgive yourself and grow from them?
- Which of those experiences did you use wisely? How did that contribute to your voice today?

As I wrote this chapter, I saw with fresh eyes that God had been giving me "voice lessons" all along so that I could grow in using my voice for the better. Isaiah 30:21 reminds me to tune in to God's voice for direction:

> Whether you turn to the right or to the left, your ears will hear a **voice** behind you, saying, "This is the way; walk in it."

CHAPTER FIVE

"Y" the "I" Mattered

No exploration of the development of my voice would be complete without the story of the spelling, or perhaps I should say *spellings,* of my name. A brief return to second grade will help set the stage.

"Sandy, how would you like to run an errand for me?" my mother asked. I leaped at the chance. Now that I was a big second grader, I reveled in the new responsibilities entrusted to me. "I had some pictures developed and they are ready," she said. "I'd like you to ride your bike to the drugstore and pick them up."

She didn't have to ask me twice! I bolted for the garage, then confidently pedaled my way through our neighborhood in Phoenix, Arizona, to the drugstore. Walking through the tall doors, though, and approaching the lady standing behind the high counter, I suddenly felt a bit small and timid.

"How can I help you, dear?" she asked, looking down at me.

"I'd like to pick up some pictures," I said quietly.

"Your last name?" she said.

"Patty."

I'll never forget her saying (in that sweet, condescending voice that grownups can have), "No, honey, your *last* name."

I said (kindly, I hoped), "Ma'am, that *is* my last name."

It has been a lifetime issue. Soon after that, when asked, our family began to qualify our last name by saying, "It's Patty. Just like a girl's first name. P-a-t-t-y." Fewer questions arose when we took the time to spell it out.

I remember my dad telling a funny story of when he played football in college. He was the quarterback for the Anderson College Ravens in Anderson, Indiana, and one of his teammates, the wide receiver, had the last name of Judy. They shared the frustration of name confusion. During one game, my dad stepped back into the pocket to throw a pass to his wide receiver, and the announcer said, "It looks like a long pass from Patty to Judy. Wait a minute! Are we playing a powder puff game here?" While the crowd had their laugh, the pass was completed, and the Ravens went on to win the game.

My first name has had its complications as well. I was born Sandra Faye Patty on July 12, 1956, to Ronald Eugene Patty and Carolyn Faye Tunnell Patty. But here's the problem when you have a last name that could be a first name—people often called me Patty. It used to bug me so much more than it does now. I finally came to understand why people do this after I met a piano player in Nashville several years ago. His name is Bill George. For some reason, I kept calling him George instead of Bill. (Ha—really!) I couldn't believe I made the mistake more than once! All that's to say, I get it now. I understand how confusing it can be to remember which name is the first and which is the last.

It's still kind of funny to me when I'm doing a concert and some very sweet person hollers, "We love you, Patty." Really? The sentiment means so much, and I don't call them out, but I'm not gonna lie. I sometimes want to shout back, "If you love me, then please learn my name."

Even though my birth certificate says Sandra, I always went by the popular shortened version, Sandy. My parents spelled it Sandy—with a *y*. But somewhere along the way, in either sixth or seventh grade, I wanted to change the spelling, so I replaced the *y* with an *i*. It just looked cool to me. So my name became Sandi (with an *i*) Patty (with a *y*).

That was how I spelled my name throughout junior high and high school, and I kept it when, in 1974, I moved on to Anderson College in Indiana. (Yep. Dad and Mom's alma mater. Even my maternal grandfather had studied there.) For a brief time, while in high school, I had thought about attending UCLA and majoring in musical theater. I'd also often dreamed of working at Disneyland as one of the Kids of the Kingdom—the enchanting, high-energy singing and dancing group that performed in the park dressed in matching outfits. By the time I graduated high school, I'd returned to the dream I'd had since childhood—to study music and become a music teacher. Anderson College was the place for me, I thought.

Once I moved there, the short-lived boldness of high school vanished. I was an introvert thrust into a world where I knew no one. Lonely and voiceless once more, within weeks I was terribly homesick. Over the phone, I convinced my family that I wanted to move back home at Christmas break. I reasoned that Anderson was expensive and that I could attend San Diego State University for far less money. My parents agreed that when the semester ended at Christmas break, I could return home. They even booked some family concerts for 1975 in anticipation of my joining them.

However, by the time Christmas rolled around, my homesickness had passed. I wanted very much to stay at Anderson, but I'd committed to San Diego State and to performing with my family. I believed it would have been wrong of me to change plans again, and so I kept my desires to myself and rejoined the family.

Kingdom Dreams

I was enrolled in the music program at SDSU for two and a half years. During that time, I couldn't help but see posted flyers advertising auditions for Disney's Kids of the Kingdom. Memories of being enthralled by the entertainers during my countless trips to Disneyland over the years reignited my old dream of being a voice in that awesome group. Besides, what better way to help pay for my college education, right?

The audition required both singing and dancing. I felt confident in my singing, but I knew that dancing wasn't my strongest skill. Still, I mustered my courage and headed to Anaheim with high hopes. There I attended the training session to learn the required dance, then joined the fifty to seventy-five other hopefuls all waiting for a turn to audition.

One by one we gave our names, danced as taught, and sang the required song. I did my very best on the dance. Then, as I was singing, my heart soared at the sight of one of the judges breaking into a smile and another folding down the edge of my application. I returned home filled with confidence and waited for the promised letter that was to come in a few weeks announcing whether I'd been accepted. Week one came and went. Week two. Week three.

Every day, I rushed to the mailbox to find nothing. After week four, I called the information number, worried my letter had been lost.

"Oh yes, Sandi Patty. I remember you," the woman said. "What a voice!" My heart skipped a beat. She remembered my name! "However, your dancing was a little weak and we felt like you were carrying a little too much weight. I'm sorry, Sandi, we just can't use you."

I wasn't good enough. Again. The words *thick* and *chubby* leaped from my high school memories to front and center, joining other words like *fat* and *ugly* and *unworthy* and *unwanted*. It didn't matter that I could sing powerfully. I wasn't enough.

It's hard even now to find adequate words to describe my devastation at that rejection. It went far beyond lacking a skill or falling short of a particular look. This huge "no" struck me at the core of my identity. I was shattered. If my singing voice wasn't enough to override those things I lacked, then what was left of me? Nothing. I felt invisible. Worthless. The little six-year-old girl inside of me stepped out of the shadows, took center stage, and named me wrong, damaged, a failure, guilty. I stayed in my room, crying for days. Though my loving family spoke tender words of comfort, I had nothing to say to them. My identity was lost in my grief. Heartbroken and hopeless, I decided to leave California and return to Anderson College.

God, of course, knew what I did not. His plans for me were about to unfold, and it took this Disney rejection to send me on his path, which began at Anderson. His purpose for me was not meant to be revealed in the rush of one acceptance letter. He did, indeed, have a plan for me to sing for the kingdom. Not Disney's kingdom but his.

New Beginnings

Once back at Anderson, I hung out my shingle as a piano teacher to help pay for school and took on a number of young pupils. One day I received a phone call from none other than Gloria Gaither. I knew of Bill and Gloria, of course. They were considered pioneers in the Christian music industry, were alums of Anderson, and Bill was on the board of directors. But the fact that Gloria knew my name came as quite a shock. She wanted to know if I would take on two of their children as piano students. Yes!

At Anderson, my name also was circulated to sing at small events such as ladies' luncheons at the country club, Christmas banquets for organizations, and other local events. I grew used to people saying my first and last name as if it were one word. Like in the South when people are called Barbara Jean or Suzanne Marie, I became SandiPatty (and I type it that way because that's how it sounded to me).

I also sang a lot on campus for various school events, and because many of my friends kept saying to me, "You need to make an album," I finally decided to do just that. With tremendous financial help from my parents, I made an album titled *For My Friends*. My name on that first album was Sandi (with an *i*) Patty (with a *y*).

At that time, my parents joined Bill Glass, former pro football player for the Cleveland Browns, at his crusades. Mom and Dad ran the musical portion of each event, and Bill preached. From time to time, they invited me to be the special musical guest, and I got to sell my little album afterward. To my amazement, people asked me to come to their church for a concert or to sing a special or two with their choirs—even churches that weren't in Anderson, Indiana. So while I was still in college, I did a few concerts here and there.

Meanwhile, I was also doing a lot of studio work at Bill and Gloria Gaither's studio in Alexandria, Indiana, which was about a ten-minute drive from Anderson. I sang backup on several albums. I also traveled to Indianapolis, where I sang a ton of sessions for commercials—jingles mostly. The pay was great and helped me fund my schooling. One of the engineers liked my singing and my work ethic, so he gave a copy of my *For My Friends* album to Phil Brower, who was A & R (artist and repertoire) for Singspiration music—a division of Zondervan publishing at the time.

Phil called me one fall day in 1978 to talk about my becoming an artist with their record label. I invited him to a Bill Glass Crusade, where I was the special music guest for the evening, and he agreed to come. Phil was complimentary of what he heard, and as he talked with my parents and me afterward, he invited me to come to Grand Rapids, Michigan, to talk more about being a Singspiration artist. I explained that I was about to be married in November and timidly asked Mr. Brower if I could wait to come up to Grand Rapids once I had gotten married and settled into that life. He was kind and gracious and said yes. He waited until the first week of January to call to arrange for my husband and me to meet him in Michigan. I love that Phil Brower! To this day he is one of the good guys.

My husband and I drove up to Grand Rapids and began conversations about what it might be like to be a recording artist. Who would produce? What songs would we choose? I had met a man named David Clydesdale while recording at the Gaithers' studio. David was one of the staff orchestrators and arrangers for Singspiration. It just seemed to be a natural fit for David and me to begin working together along with Neal Joseph, a friend and up-and-coming producer from Anderson College. And so it began—the preparation for my first album with a record label. The label was called Milk and Honey. (Wayne Watson and Twila Paris were also on that label at one time.) The process from start to finish was at least eight months. (Probably longer, but my memory is shorter these days!)

As production neared its end, I counted the days until I would hold the album in my hands. As requested, I kept Singspiration informed of my performance schedule as the release day drew closer so I would be able to sell the new album as soon as it was ready. The day finally came. The first boxes of my debut album would arrive at a church in Ohio. There I was to meet up with my parents to perform as a special guest in one of the follow-up concerts to a Bill Glass Crusade.

When we arrived, Mom, Dad, and I excitedly gathered around and Dad cut the box open.

And that's when I saw it.

My name was misspelled on the album.

Sandi Patti. Patti with an *i* instead of a *y*. My heart sank.

The album itself was beautiful. The cover had a lovely little picture of me with a big ol' flower in my hair. For a moment, there was silence. My dad spoke first, ever the positive one. "It looks like a beautiful box of candy."

But I was looking at this sweet "box of candy" and thinking, *My name is spelled wrong on my debut professional album? Seriously?* The spelling of my name had always been a big issue. And now we had it wrong . . . again. What to do?

"Mom, does it bother you that my name is spelled wrong?" I asked.

Precious Mom. "I think it's cute with the two *i*'s."

The simple truth is I didn't know how to speak up for myself.

I had not yet found and uncovered my voice as an adult—not even a little bit. I'd grown comfortable and even confident with my stage identity, but my offstage identity was still shaky at best.

Then the self-talk began. *They've printed so many copies. Who am I to ask for them to correct it? I'm nobody. I can't possibly ask them to go through the expense of discarding the first printing. I should just roll with it.*

I couldn't even imagine causing other people so much trouble (not to mention the cost!) to fix the mistake, not even over my name, my identity. So I let that mistake stand for years and years. I signed autographs and copied the misspelling. The topic would come up from time to time in interviews, but I laughed it off and never made a big deal about it. But it did bother me. A lot. This snowball was rolling downhill and fast. I ended up making subsequent albums, and I allowed the mistake to remain, loud and proud. How could I change it after letting it go before? Who was I to challenge it?

I believed what was important to me didn't matter. My voice didn't matter. The irony is obvious, since this album was filled with my *voice.*

I took the stage that night. As always, I sang my heart out. I couldn't speak my mind, but I sure could sing my heart. I sang to the God I loved. I worshiped, and I did my very best to usher the entire audience into worship of the mighty God I adored. But inside, behind that powerful singing voice, I knew that my timid identity was cowering in the shadows, sad that my *name,* my *identity,* was in hiding.

I still felt voiceless.

Discovering Your Voice

Everyone's past is marked with disappointments and unrealized expectations. Now is your opportunity for the older, wiser you to bring some new perspective and see the bigger picture. See if the following questions help you to face your tomorrows expectantly.

- When and where has your voice been challenged and you remained silent? Can you identify steps you can take to stand firm on your identity whenever and wherever it is challenged in the future?
- Think back over some key moments in your life. Were there some that God used to help you define yourself and your value?
- Consider a few major disappointments when a "no" dashed your dreams. Now, in retrospect, can you find God's "yes" that was about to take you in a new direction?

If the older, wiser Sandi Patty could speak to the young, heartbroken Sandi in the days after the Disney disappointment, or in the aftermath of the misspelled name at the launch of her recording career, I would assure her that one day she would discover the power of living *expectantly* and in her true *identity*. Psalm 5:3 still reminds me how important it is to wait on God in full expectation that he will accomplish his perfect will in our lives:

> In the morning, Lord, you hear my **voice**;
> > in the morning I lay my requests before you
> > and wait expectantly.

I pray that you will use your voice to lay your requests before the Lord and wait with anticipation for God's best to be revealed in your life. He is worthy of your trust.

CHAPTER SIX

He Loves Me, He Loves Me Not

"Twinkle, twinkle," I sang softly to the expectant audience. I was in my first semester at Anderson, and I'd been asked by one of the local social clubs to do a mini-concert for them. I'd been given carte blanche to perform whatever songs I wanted and had included pieces recorded by a wide variety of stars, such as Barbra Streisand, Donna Summer, and Andrae Crouch. With a full band, background singers, and a brass section, I was having a ball. One of the novelty pieces I was singing was a musical variation on the song "Twinkle, Twinkle, Little Star." It started as one normally hears the childhood favorite, but then changed keys and went into a jazz version. The last part of the medley was very classical, in the key of C, and I treated it operatically and ended on a high C.

Little did I know that Greta Dominic was in the audience. Mrs. Dominic was a phenomenal voice teacher (who had been a fantastic performer in her day), and I was privileged that year to be under her instruction—my first ever formal voice lessons. I was in awe of her ability not only to sing but to bring out the best voices of her students. Thus far, though, we had struggled a bit with my voice. She heard my range as more of a mezzo-soprano, so the literature we'd been doing was in the lower notes. It was great literature and I loved it, but it didn't feel comfortable to me, yet I could not explain why.

Had I known that Mrs. Dominic was listening that night, I would have been a self-conscious bundle of nerves. Fortunately, I didn't know until the concert came to a close and I began to meet and greet a few people backstage. That was when I saw Mrs. Dominic out of the corner of my eye, and she was making a beeline straight to me. My first thought was that she was going to scold me for doing pop music, because voice teachers at the university level are notorious for not approving of their students "ruining" their voices by singing pop music. I braced myself as she approached. But the next thing I knew, I was locked in her enthusiastic embrace.

"Sandi! Where did *that* voice come from?" Her excitement colored not only her tone but her face as well. "Starting with your next lesson, we are going to find *that* voice. I didn't know you had that in you. Brava, Sandi, bra-va!"

A thrill shot through me. *She's pleased with me. More than pleased!* I thought. *I can't believe how excited she is.* I felt so cared about and was deeply touched. She had truly heard my potential. I can't help but smile every time I recall that sweet moment.

What I didn't understand then was that although, in my mind, I knew she was validating my *singing* voice, my heart took it as validation of my whole self, because singing was my only point of confidence and identity. My true identity still lacked a voice and desperately needed the validation she gave me that night.

Her words have come back to me many times over the years as

I've thought about and struggled to find my true inner voice and hoped for it to be a voice of strength, confidence, and the assurance that I was lovable and loved.

Everyone but Me

Fast-forward to the end of my junior year at Anderson. One day, the phone rang.

"Hi, Sandi, this is Bill Gaither."

By this time our paths had crossed numerous times, not only because I taught piano to two of the Gaither children and worked in their studio but also because Bill and Gloria had heard me sing at a number of school and local events. Now Bill was about to take our connection to a whole new level. I couldn't believe my ears as he told me they were embarking on a nationwide tour and asked if I'd like to go on the road with them as one of their background singers.

"Wow, Bill, let me pray about it," I said. In the next breath, I declared, "Yes!" I was unbelievably honored that they asked.

I traveled with them during my senior year as much as my school schedule allowed. I continued to travel with them over the following three to four years, during which time I got married, my Singspiration album released, and I was being requested more and more for small concerts of my own. On the outside, I appeared confident and well grounded, and indeed, when it came to my singing, I was. Yet deep inside, where no one could see and where I barely dared to look, I still felt damaged and invisible.

One song brought this point home time and time again. At nearly every appearance, we sang the song "I Am Loved" by Bill and Gloria Gaither. As I sang it, I wanted the listeners to hear and understand the words—that they were loved by God, who knows them best, and who through the sacrifice of his Son bore deep scars to express that love. I believed those words with all my heart. Yet I slowly became painfully aware that I believed they were true for everyone but me. For me, the words rang hollow—a head knowledge I'd heard since childhood rather than a truth that penetrated my deepest self. I didn't feel loved or lovable.

I learned to resign myself to the fact that while I could tell everyone else, through song, that they were loved by God, I didn't, couldn't, really count on that love for myself. I knew in my head that God loved me, but I really didn't know it in my heart. I didn't know how to apply or experience a love that seemed meant for everyone else but me. I was too damaged, my soul too hidden away to be touched and seen and loved. And so I hid behind the music. I feared that if someone *saw* me, really saw the *internal* me, they would know what a farce I was. How could someone like me be loved by the God of the universe? How could I matter to him? Because I saw only my wounds and my scars, I was certain that was all he saw as well.

A Plate of Shame

Just as my career was spiraling upward, my battle with food was spiraling downward. I will name it for what it is—addiction. I didn't see and understand that at the time, of course. That realization took a few years of additional struggle. The childhood and adolescent issues I had with food and weight, beginning at age six with the sexual abuse, had continued to plague me through college. I turned to food for comfort, to soothe my feeling of being damaged goods, to ease my angst, to compensate for my loneliness, to try to fill the empty places inside of me.

Addiction is very good at one thing—it distracts. It keeps us distracted so that it can destroy. In my case, it destroyed hope. I truly became hopeless in my battle with weight, to the point of believing I was powerless over my appetite and size. When one is without hope, there is no reason to try. And so the cycle just went deeper and deeper, growing worse as I believed the lie that I was not worthy of being healthy.

Addiction is cruel and vicious, and it won't let go of you; you have to let go of it. But I didn't see or understand that as a young, hidden, voiceless woman. Instead I became hopelessly caught in the tangled net that every addict knows too well.

Outwardly I pretended that life was good. I sang my heart out, every inch of me wanting my listeners to experience the love of God and a deeper faith in him, then I'd step off the stage feeling on the outside of that love, believing it was beyond my reach. I projected confidence and joy to others while inside I felt dry and lifeless. Everything I exuded declared that my life was good, my career was good, my marriage was good, while the hidden Sandi, voiceless and alone and unworthy, cried silently in the shadows.

Hurt People Hurt *People*

Going into my marriage to John, I remember thinking, *I'm so glad I don't have any preconceived ideas about what marriage should look like.* I remember even thinking in the back of my mind somewhere,

Of course he'll be just like my dad, right? Wrong on both counts. We actually had conflict (of course), and I didn't know what to do about it. I had never *ever* seen conflict or conflict resolution between my parents, so I assumed all conflict was my fault. I knew it. If I could just be sensitive enough or kind enough or skinny enough or loving enough, I could head off all these conflicts. They wouldn't happen if I could do better. So I put all my effort into trying to do and be better.

When broken people enter into a marriage and don't get help in healing their brokenness, they create a broken marriage. Clearly, I was broken. So many nights I would cry my eyes out while hiding in the bathroom so my husband wouldn't hear me.

God, show me how I am wrong, and then show me how to fix it, I would pray. Because I took the blame (in my mind), I believed it was up to me to fix it privately. I didn't know how to even begin a conversation of healing.

I had become so adept at stuffing and hiding my negative thoughts and feelings that not even my closest loved ones—my husband, my parents, my dearest friends—knew my struggles. When my self-loathing and sad thoughts and feelings came bubbling to the surface, I'd stuff them back down. But there's only so much room to store painful stuff in the deep cavern of feelings. Sooner or later, it all comes vomiting up. And it's uglier than ever because it has been sitting there festering all this time. It has become infected and poisoned. So a simple thought or feeling that might have been harmless before now has all this junk attached to it, and it spews all over everything. For me, this included my marriage to John.

John knows this about himself now, but back then he wasn't aware that he had a personality that so wanted the best for everyone around him that he would often go immediately to the critique of them or their behavior, bypassing the gentle words that are so needed for real change to take place. In his brokenness, he would begin with a critique of me. I would stay silent and swallow his criticism. In my own brokenness, I interpreted his words as, "Hush. Your voice is not valuable or even necessary." So rather than resolving issues, we multiplied our problems. This was a vicious cycle that, as a married couple, we were never able to navigate our way through successfully.

We Shall Behold Him

After I toured with the Gaithers for a year or so, they were gracious enough to allow me not only to sing backup vocals but also to sing a solo at the end of each concert. That song, written by the inimitable Dottie Rambo, was brand new at the time and was called "We Shall Behold Him." To this day, it is still one of the most requested songs that I have been privileged to sing.

Singing that song truly opened doors for me to step into the next season of my life—being a professional singer. That decision meant putting the dream of teaching music to the side, although teaching has always been my heartbeat—even when recording or sharing in concert. I've always wanted to teach and influence, to have whatever I do *matter,* not just in the moment but tomorrow, and the next day. And so, though I decided to step through the doors God opened for me to perform rather than teach music, I still wanted to be teaching—teaching the truth. And singing "We Shall Behold Him" was and is a glorious truth to teach.

From the first time I sang that song, my spirit soared with anticipation of that day when I would behold God in person.

That anticipation is why I am moved by the song more deeply than I can express. Even in my brokenness, I knew that one day I would stand face to face with God Almighty, and there in his presence I would finally know complete and total love. Though I couldn't feel his love then and there in my brokenness, I knew that when I came face to face with God, I would know that love firsthand. To this day, when I sing those words, I am praying that every listener might join me in anticipation of that great moment. And today, as I write these words, I am praying that every reader may know with absolute assurance that "we shall behold him, Savior and Lord."

Discovering Your Voice

Hymns and spiritual songs are a rich resource for inspiration. Allow these questions to help you tap into God's wisdom for you:

- What truths does God want to impart to you that are difficult for you to fully embrace?
- What hymn or spiritual song deeply stirs you to the knowledge that you are fully loved by God?
- Look up the lyrics of that song and sing or read it aloud as a prayer that God will give you a fresh glimpse of his unshakable and eternal love for you.

When I sing "We Shall Behold Him," I feel like I am living out the words of the prophet Isaiah as written in Isaiah 40:9:

> You who bring good news to Zion,
>> go up on a high mountain.
> You who bring good news to Jerusalem,
>> lift up your **voice** with a shout,
> lift it up, do not be afraid;
>> say to the towns of Judah,
>> "Here is your God!"

I urge you to lift up your voice and declare, "Here is your God!" Don't be afraid to believe that God's love is for you personally. You shall behold his love face to face!

CHAPTER SEVEN

The Guest Room

I stood behind the stage curtain with a sense of excitement as Phil Brower of Singspiration introduced me to an audience unlike any I'd ever performed for before—Christian booksellers. The year was 1979, Singspiration had just debuted my first album, and now they were showcasing me and other Singspiration artists at the Christian Booksellers Association convention in St. Louis, Missouri. Phil was the host of the evening, and he told the audience a little about me before inviting me onstage to perform "The Day He Wore My Crown." As I took my place and scanned the audience, I was aware that if this audience liked what they heard tonight, then my album would soon be appearing in Christian bookstores across the nation. Their reception didn't disappoint.

The next day, when I took my place at the Singspiration booth to meet booksellers from across the country, I found it heartwarming to be greeted by so many good folks as their friend and partner. I was at the booth an hour or so signing and giving away copies of my album. When I finished, I was encouraged to spend some time browsing the aisles of the convention floor. This was, of course, before the days of the internet, and the convention was a critically important event for publishers and manufacturers to display their new products. I was a bit overwhelmed by the huge selection of books, Bibles, music, church supplies, and gifts the booksellers could choose from and felt honored that my album was among them.

I had just turned down a new aisle when I found myself face to face with none other than Kathie Lee Gifford. (Her married name was Johnson at the time.) I'd been a fan of hers for a long time as she was the featured singer on the game show *Name That Tune,* which I watched regularly.

Whoa! She's the first famous person I've ever met, I thought, my heart rate jumping. "Oh my goodness! You're Kathie Lee," I blurted.

She stopped and said words I did not expect. "And you are Sandi Patty. I heard you sing last night, and it was glorious!"

Wait. What? She knew my name? I was stunned and grateful. We began to talk like friends as she asked about me. "Where do you live? You traveled with the Gaithers, didn't you?" I liked her immediately. She was so warm and effervescent. It turned out that we had some mutual friends. In the midst of the conversation, she said to me, "Listen, if you are ever in California, come see me in LA. Come stay with us. Anytime! Really."

I should confess here and now that I was a very naive twenty-three-year-old. If someone said to me, "I'll give you a call," or, "Let's get together," I always assumed they meant it, so my heart about leaped out of my chest at Kathie's invitation to stay at her home. She even sealed the deal by giving me her card with her personal phone number and address on it. *Is this really happening?* I wondered. I could barely believe it. Then, after affectionate goodbyes, we went our separate ways. Kathie's card, however, made it safely into my wallet.

Several months passed and I discovered that I was going to be in Los Angeles in the near future. I had held on to her business card (those who know me would assure you this is a big deal), so I wrote her a letter letting her know I'd be in her area in a few weeks and would love to take her up on her kind offer. I included my phone number, slapped a stamp on it, and into snail mail it went. I couldn't wait for her call.

But I did wait. And wait. *Hmm. Did she get my letter? Did I address it correctly? Has she retracted her invitation? Maybe I don't matter to her after all.* My travel time was quickly approaching. *Well, I'll just call her when I get out there,* I decided. (I kid you not!) Finally, once on the road, when I was within one day of arriving in LA, I pulled Kathie Lee's card out of my wallet and dialed her number.

I had expected an assistant to answer, but she answered personally.

"Oh, hi, Kathie Lee, this is Sandi Patty."

"Well, hello, my love, how are you?" *Whew,* I thought, *she remembers me!* We chatted and I asked her if she had gotten my letter.

"I'm not sure. Let me look. I've been traveling for a bit and haven't gotten my mail." After a pause she was back on the line. "Okay. It's right here." She opened it and began to read it with a "hmm-hmm" and a murmured "oh yes, we'd love it," and then she said, "Oh, you mean tomorrow. Like . . . *tomorrow,* tomorrow?" And just as I was saying yes, she read aloud, "for a week?"

And that is what it took for it to finally dawn on me that, in essence, I was showing up unannounced on her doorstep. Call it immaturity or stupidity. The thing is I hadn't felt at all smug or entitled about it. I felt honored by her invitation. I had just taken her at her word. *If you are ever in California, come see me in LA. Come stay with us. Anytime! Really.* Now here I was!

Do you know what that sweet, beautiful Kathie Lee said?

"You just come on over tomorrow, honey, and we'll figure out the rest when you get here." And the very next day I arrived with a week's worth of luggage. To this day, I still can't tell you exactly why I did it, because there is no way I would *ever* do such a thing today. No way! And if one of my adult children even hinted of doing it to someone else, I'd give them a good talking-to.

But then again, maybe I don't need that kind of unannounced wide-open hospitality now the way I needed it back then, when I didn't think I mattered much to anyone. And that is why that sweet angel named Kathie Lee has remained such a beautiful gift in my life. She welcomed me like family. She put me up in her guest room and appeared to breeze through the week as if she'd been expecting me for months and was so glad to have me. She acted as though I really mattered to her.

I didn't tell her how I'd been struggling within myself. I told no one that. I stayed as hidden as always behind my well-worn mask of confidence and positive outlook. But oh, around Kathie Lee I felt *seen.* Seen and wanted and welcomed and warmed and comforted. Her hospitableness was like a balm to my weary soul, and I savored every moment of it.

Kathie Lee has continued to be so kind to me over the years, both personally and professionally. Even three years ago, when I was ready to announce the Forever Grateful tour—my farewell tour— she invited me to her NBC show to help me announce it, letting me know this milestone in my career truly mattered to her. She really is a loving and kind and gracious woman. She inspires me to this day.

There are two specific ways Kathie Lee inspired me to emulate her voice of encouragement and hospitality—to let others know that they matter, too. The first way was through an example that Kathie gave on her thirtieth birthday. I'm not at all ashamed to say that I copied her. When I turned thirty, I threw a birthday party for myself, and I invited a number of women in my life, because *I* wanted to celebrate *them*. They were women who had helped me and continued to help shape me into the woman I am today. I gave each of them a gift and then wrote how I felt about them and what I had learned from each of them. As you can imagine, we pretty much laughed and cried together for two hours. Oh, how grateful I am to God for giving me the voice to declare their blessings in my life!

The second way I was inspired to emulate Kathie Lee began in Paris, France. I have been privileged to sing at an amazing church in Paris over the last several years. I have been there three times, and it continues to be one of the highlights of my professional life. At the church, there was a young woman I noticed the first time I visited and each time since. As the worship leader, she vigorously sang with all the musicians during the music and worship part of the service. She wordlessly communicated with the band regarding "one more time" and "last chorus," which the leader should always do. For a few lines within a song, she would step out and sing solo. And mercy, the girl can sing!

During my second visit, she shared with me how someone had given her my music when she was younger. There wasn't a lot of Christian music in French, and she very much wanted to be a Christian singer. Through an interpreter, she told me how the songs I had been honored to sing had meant so much to her. This past time (my third), I had the privilege of going to the Paris church again, where I got to watch her and leaned in to really listen to her heart. Such beauty and professionalism. Such a wonderful voice and a more gracious heart. Afterward I found myself saying to her, "Hey, why don't you come see us when you are in the United States? You can stay with us in Oklahoma."

Now, those who know me know I don't like spontaneity. Not even a tiny bit. I need a plan. And I need time and a process and warning. But in that moment, I was totally spontaneous. I wanted her to know that she mattered—she mattered in the kingdom, her gift mattered to the church at large, and she mattered to me.

She said to me, "Really? When?"

It was on! I remembered, of course, my twenty-three-year-old self saying to Kathie Lee, "Hey, I'm coming tomorrow," so how could I possibly take back the invitation?

Okay, I thought, *this is happening.* She suggested the first part of September, and I accepted, not knowing when we made those plans that Don was going to have to have knee surgery. *But hey,* I thought, in the spirit of Kathie Lee, *here we go!*

She came and we had a busy but wonderful week, and I was deeply blessed. She reminded me of many things, including how fortunate we are in America. "The kingdom is open here in America," she kept saying. "In France, it's closed." She marveled at the vibrancy of the church in America. She even went with me on a "one-off" (a stand-alone concert that isn't connected to a tour), where I had her sing. The people went crazy over her. She also sang at our church the following Sunday, and our people loved her so much. She loved them all right back.

It was, obviously, a bit of a hectic week, but I wouldn't change a thing. When I took her to the airport, there were tears in our eyes.

I thought I was blessing her with my invitation, but as it turned out, *she* was blessing *me*.

Since I have found my voice, I've tried to tell Kathie Lee over the years just how much she has meant to me. That she would let a naive young girl just show up on her doorstep, and give her love and hospitality for a week. I want her to know that what she did *mattered* to a voiceless girl suffering in silence.

Discovering Your Voice

Hospitality, I have discovered, always matters. Kathie Lee's love and fellowship were a precious step toward my finding a voice to emulate.

- Think about a person God has placed in your life who makes you feel that you matter.
- If you were to emulate another believer in demonstrating value and worth to others, who would that be and why?
- If hospitality is difficult for you, what steps can you take to start small (with just snack or dessert or coffee), knowing what a difference you can make in someone else's life just by extending an invitation and listening?

In John 14, after the Last Supper, Jesus had an amazing conversation with his disciples as he offered them comfort and prepared them for what was about to happen. Though they didn't yet understand what was to come, he was clearly speaking words that when they looked back would take on their full meaning. I adore the words he spoke to them in verses 2 and 3 (NKJV):

In My Father's house are many mansions; if it were not so, I would have told you. I go to prepare a place for you. And if I go and prepare a place for you, I will come again and receive you to Myself; that where I am, there you may be also.

(You will notice that I didn't use a "voice" verse this time. This verse was simply too perfect not to use!)

Today, hear the voice of your Savior saying those very words to *you*. You matter to Jesus. He looks forward to your arrival and is preparing a guest room just for you.

CHAPTER EIGHT

Critical Conversations

John and I had our eleventh anniversary dinner all planned. We'd hired a sitter for our three children for a relaxing November evening out at a nice restaurant, followed by a movie. The year was 1989. Anna, our oldest, was five, and our twins, Jonathan (Buddy) and Jennifer (Jenni), would be turning two on the thirtieth of the month. Our youngest, Erin, was still cuddled up in my womb awaiting her January birthday, so we took her with us.

On the drive to the restaurant, we decided that we'd do something we rarely did. We would leave the mobile phone in the car. Mobile phones weren't terribly common in 1989, and they were big. I mean *big!* I carried mine around in a case that I jokingly called the phone suitcase. Its size certainly earned it its name. I usually carried it with me so I could be available to the kids and to my staff (my career had really ramped up by then and travel was frequent). But we wanted this evening to be about the two of us, not the kids or business. Surely a few hours out of touch wouldn't hurt.

By the time the movie was over, we'd been unavailable for four hours, so I decided to call home and check in on the kids, believing they'd be sound asleep. The moment the sitter answered, however, I heard panic in her voice and felt a rush of adrenaline.

"Sandi, Jonathan had an accident and we had to take him to the ER."

I went numb.

"We've tried to call you multiple times, but you must have had the phone off."

John fired up the car and zipped out of the parking lot while I stayed on the line, my heart thumping wildly as she explained what had happened. We had a heavy wooden hall tree with metal hooks that stuck out for hanging coats and hats. Each of the kids' winter coats hung on one of the hooks, and each coat had mittens dangling from them—the kind that were attached to a long piece of yarn threaded through the sleeves. One little mitten from Jonathan's coat was hanging right where he could reach it. He started to tug on the mitten, but his coat didn't come loose. So he pulled harder and harder until the entire piece of furniture came down on him, and one of the metal hooks hit him on the left side of the head.

His head began to bleed from a gash, so the quick-thinking babysitter called Betty, our daytime nanny, who rushed over with her husband and took Jonathan to the ER.

"The good news is that he's already back home and sound asleep," the sitter reported. The ER doctor had put four stitches in the gash and sent him home. As relieved as I was to hear that he was okay, I felt a desperate need to see my little boy with my own eyes. I was already "shoulding" myself. *I should have taken the phone into the restaurant and movie. I never should have gone out and left the children. I should have called multiple times during the evening. I never should have had a hall tree. I should have made sure that nothing dangled from the tree in reach of the toddlers.* Even as I'm writing this, years later, it is tempting to wonder what I could have done differently.

The Long Night

The drive home felt like it took an eternity. When we finally arrived, I rushed to Buddy's room to see for myself that he was okay. He was sleeping soundly. I examined the stitches, and it looked like the doctor had patched him up nicely. A wave of relief washed over me. Throughout the night, about once an hour, I tiptoed into his room to check on him. As the night wore on, I noticed that he became a little restless. As I looked closer at the stitched-up cut, it looked to me like it was oozing. There was no blood flowing from the wound, but a combination of blood and clear liquid seemed to be slowly seeping from it.

That's probably normal, I told myself, so I decided to check on him again in another hour. This time, the oozing was more prevalent. I called our pediatrician's answering service at 3:00 a.m., and he was kind enough to call me right back. He asked me to keep an eye on it for another hour or two. Even though Buddy still seemed a bit restless, he appeared to be sleeping soundly. I continued to check on him. I couldn't go back to sleep even when I tried. The wound continued to leak and ooze.

Around 7:00 a.m., I checked on him again, and I will never forget what I saw. There was Buddy, sitting up—sort of. He was slumped in the corner of his crib, and the entire left side of his body looked like he'd had a stroke. The left side of his face was drooping. His left arm was motionless. Even though his eyes were open, he was unresponsive. Usually when I went to get Buddy in the morning, he would be standing up, smiling, and babbling—sometimes with a few real words thrown in—reaching for me to lift him from his crib. Not this time. I tried various things to get his attention, but nothing worked. By this time I was frantic. We called some nearby family, and bless their hearts, they immediately came over to stay with Anna and Jenni while we raced Buddy back to the ER.

The emergency staff immediately took us back, and after giving Buddy some sedation, they did a CT scan of his head. They even allowed me in the technician's room along with our pediatrician and the chief radiologist. As the scan displayed on-screen, I heard a quiet "oh no" from the pediatrician. The monitor showed massive bleeding on his brain. I'm sure what took place next happened very fast, but it remains in my memory as a movie playing in slow motion. The doctors called for an ambulance and asked which Indianapolis hospital we wanted to take Buddy to. He needed emergency brain surgery, and they were unequipped to handle such serious head trauma.

My mind was spinning. "I don't know anything about those two hospitals. If this were your son, where would you take him?" I asked. Without hesitation he gave me an answer, and they prepped my precious almost-two-year-old to be transferred by ambulance to that hospital. I was allowed to ride in the front of the ambulance, and John followed in the car. I believe I held my breath for a good part of the drive, because I recall feeling breathless all the way there. Breathless, but not voiceless. Not now.

My usual timidity didn't surface at all. I felt like a mama bear protecting her cub.

I kept turning around and asking the EMT, "Is he still breathing?"

Then I prayed aloud, "Dear Lord, save my son. Spare his life. Get him into surgery in time." Between desperate prayers, I cried, then prayed some more.

At one point I turned to the EMT who was driving and asked her what would happen when we arrived at the hospital. In her steady, calming voice, she walked me through the intake process and then warned me that they would most likely whisk Buddy away to get him to surgery quickly. I so appreciated her kindness that day in just letting me know what to expect. She kept to the facts and didn't offer false promises or hope. We both knew what was happening—my son's brain was bleeding, and every minute was more serious than the last. Each time I looked back at him, he was ashen, and his left side still drooped like that of a stroke victim.

When we arrived at the hospital, I got out of the ambulance cab and rushed to the back, where they were removing Buddy on a gurney. He had all kinds of tubes in him and was still unresponsive.

"But his vitals are good," said the EMT.

I clung to those five words.

Conversation in the Chapel

The team of doctors and nurses couldn't have been kinder. They explained their plan of draining the excess blood from Buddy's brain, then finding and stopping the source of the bleeding. They warned me they'd be shaving the left side of his head. When the OR nurse said it was time to take him to the operating room, I felt like I was relinquishing my son to her, not knowing whether I'd ever see him alive again. It was a horrible feeling.

A few minutes later, I was surprised when one of the nurses returned from the OR holding a baggie, which she handed to me. It was filled with Buddy's gorgeous curly red hair. None of the serious, scary moments in the hospital so far had made me cry, but this kind gesture was the one thing that slipped through that little crack in the dam of tears I was desperately trying to hold back.

I wept. I wept for the unknown that was soon to be. I wept for the what-ifs and should-haves. I wept in fear for my son's precious life.

Through my tears, I found my way to the little hospital chapel, where I waited for Buddy to come out of surgery. I needed some conversation with my God—private, uninterrupted, sacred conversation.

And I didn't feel voiceless. Not at all. I had no shortage of words and no reticence to speak them. I knew my heavenly Father was present and with me, fully available, loving me, loving Buddy. My prayer was simple. "God, help me trust you, even when I may not understand." That didn't mean I had peace in that moment. I didn't. I was, quite frankly, irritated with God. "Why?" Not a question that God is unfamiliar with, I'm sure. "What next?" Another question our Lord knows well.

Several years earlier, my younger brother, Craig, had been in a serious car crash that resulted in a head injury. He was in a coma for weeks, followed by many months of physical therapy. Still, years later, there were issues that my brave, sweet brother dealt with daily as the result of his brain trauma. So I knew that head injuries are serious. Even if one survives a head injury, there are often lifetime consequences that must be dealt with.

Instead of being the timid little girl inside of me, hiding in the shadows, who so often in personal crisis couldn't find her words, afraid of what God would do if she used them, I was bold in approaching the throne of grace, confident of being heard and loved. Not confident in God's answer—I honestly didn't know whether he would spare my son, nor what would follow if he did—but confident that somehow, mysteriously, I could trust God and would follow him through this. If ever I needed proof that faith is a gift given by God rather than mustered up on my own, that conversation in the chapel demonstrated to me that God had given me the faith to believe in him and his love. Even if I didn't know his answer, even if I didn't know the "why" or the "what next," I knew I could lift my voice to him and he would hear me. And so I prayed and wept and prayed some more.

I'm not sure how long I was there, but eventually I joined John back in the waiting room where we waited. And waited. And waited. Finally, an attendant came to guide us to a small consultation room. I worried that you get sequestered there only if the doctor is going to be giving bad news. We waited what seemed like an eternity, even though it was only a few minutes. The doctor arrived and explained to us what had happened. The impact of the blow Buddy had received the night before had chipped a piece of his skull and pushed it into his brain. This had caused a slow bleed, and that's why there was no evidence of it the night before.

He explained that they removed a saucer-sized piece of Buddy's skull so they could access and remove the small chipped piece. Once they had that piece in hand, they worked to carefully drain the remaining pooled blood and were pleased when they saw that the bleeding had stopped. They stitched him back up and then stapled his skull back on his head. Now we would simply have to "wait and see."

Jonathan was transferred to the pediatric ICU, where he was monitored 24/7. We were encouraged to continue to interact with him as we normally would, so we held him and spoke to him, but we were getting no response at all, which was unnerving. He would open his eyes from time to time, but it was a slow gaze that really wasn't focused on anything in particular. As each hour slipped by, my heart braced for my worst fear. I prepared my momma's heart to say goodbye to my little boy. My son. My buddy.

Lighting Up

The hospital had strollers we could borrow, so the day after Jonathan's surgery, we walked around with him a lot—all around the hospital, inside and out. We greeted other patients, pointed out trees and flowers. We listened to music on a cassette player and sang to him. Still, an unresponsive Buddy.

On day three (though it felt like one long day), I planned to take a walk with Buddy, pushing him in the stroller. We were standing by the elevator, waiting to go down so we could walk around outside a little bit. The elevator doors opened and out came a little girl in a stroller being pushed by her grandma. It took me a minute to register that this was John's mom, Grandma Doris, and she was pushing Jenni, Buddy's twin sister, in the stroller.

I don't know how to explain what happened next except to say something lit up in Buddy. Clearly recognizing his sister, he sat upright in the stroller and began "talking" to her. It was unintelligible to us, but not to Jenni. She began to babble back. Then Buddy babbled something else to her and got animated and pointed.

Doris and I looked at each other with expressions that clearly said, *What's happening?* We called the nurses so they could document what we thought we were seeing. Buddy was responding. Interacting. Buddy was getting better. When the doctor came in for rounds later that day, he said, "Well, I hear we've had a pretty interesting day around here." Although the nurses had explained to him what had happened, we couldn't help but excitedly share our own version as well. Buddy was sitting up, and as the doctor turned to interact with him, he could see that something really good was happening.

Over the next couple of days, Buddy became more and more interactive. The few words that an almost-two-year-old has in his vocabulary returned, as did his understanding and his appetite. The doctor announced that he saw no reason why Buddy couldn't go home. We were astounded. It had been less than a week since I had prepared my heart to say goodbye to my sweet son and now there was talk of taking him home! We finished up our conversation with the doctor in the hallway just outside Buddy's room, and when I stepped back in, Buddy had gotten himself into the stroller. It was obvious that he had understood the doctor when he said, "You can go home. What do you think about that?" Though several hours passed before we got checked out, Buddy never left that stroller—not once. The boy was ready to go home. The left side of his head was shaved and the staples from the surgery were still horseshoed into his scalp. He didn't care. He just wanted to go home. So home we went.

A lot of life has been lived by that almost-two-year-old boy now-thirty-year-old man who stands before me today. He is kind and considerate. He is quirky and smart. He strives to be a man of God. He is a hard worker and has learned to apply himself, even though some things have been more difficult for him than for someone who hasn't had a head injury. Some of the skills that most of us take for granted Jonathan has had to relearn.

However, singing and music—difficult for some—come as naturally to Jonathan as breathing. I like to say that Buddy *is* music. He hears music in his soul. He hears songs in his heart. And he sees the colors with which they paint the world. He writes lyrics. And when he sings, oh my, my heart sings with him. Such moments take me back every time to the memory of handing him over to the surgical nurse not knowing whether I would ever hold him again.

I know that not everyone has the same happy ending to a story like this. That is why I never ever, not for one single moment, take it for granted that I have my Buddy in my life. Jonathan gives back to this world far more than he takes. Though I know he will always struggle with some life stuff that challenges him, Jonathan always leaves people and situations better than he found them.

When he sings, there is hope and there is life. And this mother never stops using her voice to tell God that she is grateful that he heard her pain, anger, and desperation—and surrender—that day in the chapel. And the boldness I demonstrated that day is a reminder to me that even though I might often feel hidden, there lives inside of me a child of God confident in the listening ear and living presence of God—not just for everyone else but for me as well.

Discovering Your Voice

Psalm 27:7 is a plea that I know God always answers:

> Hear my **voice** when I call, LORD;
>> be merciful to me and answer me.

The important thing is to *use* our voices to call on the Lord no matter what the circumstances! He eagerly listens when we share our truest hearts with him.

- How comfortable are you with having conversations with God when you are in distress? When you are celebrating?
- Are you able to trust God to hear your prayers and act in love on your behalf, even if things don't go as you'd hoped?

David's prayers recorded in the Psalms demonstrate how freely we can express the full range of our emotions to God—our anger, our fears, our questions and heartbreak, our joys and praises. If ever you feel voiceless in your conversations with God, find some psalms that express what you are feeling and read them aloud. As you fill your heart with God's Word, not only will your trust grow but so will your relationship with him.

CHAPTER NINE

Blisters and Calluses

"Hi, Sandi. How has your week been?" I eagerly snuggled into a chair for my weekly thirty-minute phone chat with Bev, my Bible Study Fellowship leader. Her calls had come to mean so much to me. Clearly, God in his omniscience had known that at this chaotic point in my life, I needed to be grounded in his Word through Bible Study Fellowship (BSF, a remarkable ministry of in-depth Bible study) and mentored by Bev. She never knew what my answer to her weekly question might be. So much was going on, I often didn't know where to start.

A tremendous number of events—good, bad, wondrous, and horrendous—had squeezed into my life during the three or so years since Buddy's accident. On the positive side, my career was blossoming like never before. Traveling around the country for arena concert performances, new invitations pouring in, albums releasing. My sense of ministry to my audience was exhilarating and incredibly rewarding. I loved taking the stage and singing of God's love and majesty, and I truly enjoyed speaking to people after concerts, especially when they shared how their spiritual lives had been awakened in new ways as they heard me sing.

But there was a flip side. At times my career felt like a runaway train, or maybe I should say a runaway *bus,* since we used a tour bus to crisscross the country. The bus enabled us to bring the children along as we traveled, allowing for more family time—which I loved—but it also made it increasingly difficult to separate family life from work life. John was not only my husband but my manager as well, which compounded the growing conflict between us, affecting my work life and our family life in destructive ways.

More and more staff became necessary to handle the complex demands of our business, which meant employing many people to keep my crazy career afloat. I loved and appreciated these people, but I had an unhealthy sense of responsibility for them all—for their comfort, their happiness, their work satisfaction. I believed my job was to make everyone feel better—a burden I keenly felt—often at the expense of authenticity and at the expense of me. And even though I suffered a miscarriage during this time, I pushed on, not wanting to disrupt the touring.

Outwardly I pretended that I was good. Marriage was good. Life was good. Being a mom of young children was good. My career was good. I worked hard to make it look like I had it all together. I would sing from emotional depths, then leave the stage, go to my dressing room, where no one would see me, and sit in the corner and cry. I would weep tears from so deep down I honestly didn't know where they were coming from. And then I'd put the mask back on to go meet the people who were kind enough to come to the concert. When the line dwindled and the venue lights dimmed, I'd get back on the bus and do what? Eat.

The truth is I adored my kids and tried my hardest to be a good mom. But with four kids and their needs, on a bus, and a big career with lots of professional demands that never ended, I felt like there wasn't enough of me to go around. I ate, perhaps unconsciously adding pounds to make *more* of me to go around. As I grew bigger and bigger, I fell deeper and deeper into depression and despair, with only occasional glimmers of short-lived hope. The weight (literally) of all of this brought with it great shame and furthered the familiar old feelings of being fat and ugly and unworthy and hidden.

All of this had a profound effect on my inner voice. With children and staff and marriage rolling along together from city to city, there were, naturally, plenty of relational needs and demands for conflict resolution. But I was so adept at avoiding conflict that I stuffed the need to have important conversations inside, allowing problems to fester, suffocating my voice all the more.

Unlike my internal struggles, I couldn't hide my weight. So I sang louder and higher to distract people from seeing me, the real me. The stifled voice inside longed to be heard—really heard. I was caught in a vortex, a whirlwind of good and bad swirling around me and inside of me, sucking me dry. It seemed I could find no safe space.

Ironically, it was sometime during this period that my new label, Word Music, decided to brand me as *The Voice*. I didn't say a word to object, of course. How could I? I should be honored, right? So I played the part. But it pained me to no end that of all times to be dubbed *The Voice*, it should happen while I was drowning in voicelessness.

A Safe Place in the Chaos

Into this morass came Bible Study Fellowship, and with it, Bev. Two things happened at once. The first is that as I immersed myself in

God's Word, his truth penetrated my dark places, shedding light on areas that desperately needed help and healing. One thing I have seen happen over and over again is that when we draw close to God's Word, God surfaces our "stuff" that keeps us blocked spiritually. His Word loosens the grip that our wounds have on us. Our baggage becomes more obvious and more uncomfortable because we are placing so much of God's truth into our souls. My friend Marilyn Meberg says that "our wounds will come burping up to the surface."

Once I became part of BSF, my discussion leader, Bev, called me every week (as she did everyone in our group). She would begin by saying, "How has your week been?" Thirty or forty minutes later, we would end our discussion. She not only invited me to share but also really listened. I think she was the first woman in my life (who wasn't family or a close friend) who chose to come alongside and mentor me. I didn't know that word at the time, but looking back, I see that is exactly what she was doing—mentoring me by helping me process the messy intersection of my life and faith. A consistent part of my life, she demonstrated her love and care for me so unconditionally that I was able to share some of my deeply rooted wounds—a huge step I'd never taken before. She built a safe space of grace for me to express my truest voice.

As I continued BSF and talking regularly with Bev, she sensed that it might be time for me to go to counseling. I thought, at the time, that counseling is for those who are weak, lack faith, and can't get through life by themselves. God had to redirect this belief in my life. No one can make it through life by themselves. We need each other desperately. We need to hear one another's stories and to share our stories as well. Sometimes, when that need is complex and painful, a trained counselor can be a tremendous gift to help sort out truth from lies.

So there I was, in my midthirties, finally allowing some truth and vulnerability to seep through the cracks in the armor I had fashioned.

God loves you, Sandi. You personally. Not everyone except you. You! I was hearing it over and over again—from God's Word, from BSF, from Bev, from my Christian counselor—as if for the first time ever. It took me back to my old internal dialogue when I used to sing "I Am Loved" with the Gaithers.

I'm a terrible person. I'm bad. I'm ugly and fat. I've done this terrible thing and that awful thing. He couldn't possibly love me.

Eventually, I began to believe his love for me might be true. Then I would think, *Well, okay, he's God. That's his job. He's supposed to love me. He's obligated.*

Then someone whispered in my ear one day, "Honey, God *likes* you, too."

Sorry? What?

"He doesn't just love you. He likes you. He wants to be your friend."

Hold on! Honestly? God likes me? Me? What a striking concept! The names of people in my life whom I loved (maybe because I had to) but didn't actually like popped into my head. *Liking someone is a whole different thing than loving them.* (I bet you can think of people you love but don't necessarily like. You know you can. You're thinking of them right now. Hah! Gotcha!)

To be *liked* by the God of the universe? This would mean he *chooses* me. He chooses to spend time with me because he *wants* to. How is this possible? Maybe he gets a kick out of the way I sing.

Or laughs when I do something silly. Or maybe he smiles when I throw my arms around my kids. I've heard someone say, "If God had a refrigerator, your picture would be on it." I only put pictures of people on our refrigerator whom I enjoy. Could God possibly feel that way about me?

This opened up a whole new inner world for me. I wondered: If I lived every day as though I were the most loved (and liked) person in the world, how would I act differently? I'd probably not worry about my weight quite so much (although that's a never-ending struggle). I would probably worry less what other people think of me. I'd probably say hi to a perfect stranger and not be scared I'd say something wrong. I'd probably be more able to speak the truth in love. I'd probably have less fear when I go to bed at night, knowing God holds me when I'm broken. I'd probably be able to rest easier knowing that God not only has me but has my kids, too. My family, my parents. All of us.

And then it hit me—that's what Bill and Gloria's song was saying, but I had missed it back then. Yet somehow the truth got planted in my heart and bloomed at just the right time. And here it is: When I know that I am loved, I am able to *risk* (because let's face it, relationships of any kind are a risk) loving others. When I am loved, I am able to offer grace and understanding to those around me as well as to myself. To offer kindness and mercy along with truth. Because the one who knows me best loves me most! And just as amazing, he *likes* me!

Jesus' voice in John 15:15 seemed to come alive, speaking directly to me: "I no longer call you servants, because a servant does not know his master's business. Instead, I have called you friends, for everything that I learned from my Father I have made known to you."

I don't know about you, but my friends are people I like even though I don't have to. And I am God's friend.

But here's a warning: When you decide to step into God's truth and to step away from the lies you always held as truth, your world is upended. For a bit. It's confusing and it's disarming. And you may run around chasing your tail for a while. I used to get so irritated when people said that God is even in the chaos. Well, guess what? He is. And sometimes we need a good dose of chaos to shake us out of our familiar ways and wake us up to see his truth. And that is exactly where my chaos led me. Jesus was making himself *known* to me on a whole new level.

I saw my counselor in Indianapolis, and as those weeks and months became a couple of years, it became clear that the deeply broken places in my world needed to be addressed head-on and at full steam.

I have become a big fan of counseling in the last half of my life. I honestly wish I had known its value long before I hit my midthirties. In my generation of Christian women, going to a counselor was still a bit taboo and difficult to admit or talk about. I think today's generation of women really understands the importance of making sense of life while in process. Don't hesitate to use the great resource of a good counselor. The earlier in life you unpack your baggage, the better.

Pointe Shoes

As I asked God to reframe truth in my life, I began to feel a little bit more comfortable with the risk of exercising my voice and speaking my opinion. It was like trying out what would soon become my favorite comfortable pair of shoes, but first they were giving me huge blisters, and I didn't know if the pain and effort would be worth it. But the godly women who came into my life through BSF and counseling encouraged me to speak my voice. Try it out. Build up some calluses over those tender blisters.

My daughter Anna studied dance for many years. I remember the day she was finally ready to get her first pair of pointe shoes. Ah, pointe shoes—the end game for any serious dancer. It just didn't get any better than pointe shoes! She was so excited as we went to the store and she tried on a few. The expert who fit her for these special shoes gave her some pointers (ha—couldn't resist the pun!) on how to get comfortable in these shoes.

"Anna," the shoe specialist said, "these are going to take some getting used to. You're going to want to throw them away the first week. Your toes are going to hurt. Your ankles are going to ache. You are going to get blisters that will feel like they are never going to go away. You will even think about giving up your dream of being a ballerina. But it's worth it."

Sure enough, Anna got blisters that hurt so bad she was in tears at the end of dance practice. But those blisters toughened and became calluses. And Anna toughened up along the way, too. She understood that to achieve her dream, there had to be some pain involved. To this day, she takes great pride in those well-earned calluses. She refuses to get a pedicure because, as she says, "Mom, I have earned these calluses, and I don't want anyone scraping them off. They remind me that I can work hard and push through."

Yes! Let's hear it for ballet pointe shoes! Let's hear it for trying something new and allowing it to be uncomfortable—or even painful—for a while. Let's hear it for the people in our lives who cheer us on. "You've got this, girl. It's gonna be worth it."

That is what it was like for me to start uncovering my voice. Often, I've learned, the first thing that happens is that the people who have been around the voiceless person will look at her like she's crazy. "Wait, did *you* just say that?" The second thing that happens is that people will rejoice with you or they will rebel against you. The ones who rebel want things to stay the way they were. They'll actually escalate their domineering or bullying behavior to try to get you to go back to your silent ways. I confess, when others did this to me, there were times I was tempted to go back into hiding. I was getting a lot of blisters from my new shoes, and it did not feel good. And yet the more I risked using my voice, the more I reveled in the freedom of it.

At first my voice started only in my head. I'd make a comment to myself or dare to think a different opinion than what I was hearing. In time, I began thinking, *Hey, I like this opinion.* When I became braver and bolder, I began to share those "blistering" opinions with my girlfriends, many of whom said to me, "Well, hello, Sandi. It's about time!"

One example comes to mind. I was on the road performing, traveling with my kids. We had two nannies traveling with us, and we set up camp in arenas everywhere we went. The venue staff provided dressing rooms for us, and we always marked one dressing room Nursery. One day, the kids were just done with arenas and the bus. They were probably around ages eight (Anna), five and five (Buddy and Jenni), and three (Erin). They all needed some good sound sleep in a hotel.

So our tour manager arranged for hotel rooms (*always* adjoining) so that the evening would be less chaotic for the kids, for the nannies, and ultimately for me as well, because although I still worried about them, it was a different worry when they weren't onsite. The plan was that the nannies and the kids would get settled into the hotel, and I would meet them there after the show.

Late that night when I got to the hotel and checked in with the nannies, they explained to me that since there were no adjoining rooms available, they'd put the kids in a room *by themselves*. The nannies planned to stay in a room together.

Okay, so come with me here. Let's just talk about safety. The whole point of adjoining rooms was that all outside doors could be locked and yet the kids and nannies still had access *to each other*. But these two nannies had put the kids in a room by themselves with no adult present!

Here's what I said in response: "Oh, okay."

They then said to me (because I had implied permission for them to say it), "Yes, we're tired. It's so exhausting taking care of these kids on the road. But don't worry, we have a key to their room and we have their monitor so we can hear them."

I said, "I'm so sorry it has been such an inconvenience to you. Thank you. I know you work hard," blah, blah, blah. But all the while I was thinking, *That was the worst choice ever! If you had to split up, then one nanny should be with a couple of kids and the other nanny with the others. But you never should have put them in a room all by themselves!*

I didn't address the problem with the nannies. Instead, I felt sorry for the burden I had placed on them and I bunked in with the kids that night. I certainly couldn't leave them alone.

A few months later, some girlfriends and I were having lunch and I brought up this story. My three friends were horrified. They turned to me and said, "You fired them, right?"

"No, I didn't fire them." And I babbled on about how hard it was for the nannies because traveling is hard, kids are hard, and so on.

They looked at me, baffled. "Sandi, it's their *job!* You aren't there to make *their* job easier. They are there to make *your* job easier."

I was stunned. And in that split second, one of my blisters callused over and I got mad. I got mad at the nannies and their poor choice that night. And other nights, as I later found out. I asked my girlfriends (innocently) if I should talk to the nannies about this. And my friends were like, "Girl, I would have fired them! Have you not said *anything* to them?"

"No. I did not speak up."

At that moment, I could see that I hadn't used my voice. I was working hard at learning to speak up, but the blisters were still there, and they hurt. So I decided to speak directly, in person, without apology, to the nannies. I practiced with my girlfriends. With them I decided to say to the nannies, "I'm not sure what the circumstances were, but let me tell you this. Do not ever, *ever* put the kids in one room by themselves while you two are in another room needing a break. This is your *job!*" It felt so good to speak that truth aloud and for my friends to affirm my feelings and words—and then to act on them.

That's just one example, but it's indicative of the ways in which I'd been voiceless and was now beginning, just beginning, to find and use my voice.

So thanks to BSF, to God's Word, to Bev, to my counselor, and to good honest friends, I made my way through the chaos to walk in more light, to speak more truth, to risk.

But there was still plenty of darkness in my chaos. And I was about to discover just how deeply broken I really was. Every area of my life was about to come crashing down. I've been discovering, however, that it takes new eyes to recognize how God, in his grace, was and is always at work putting all the broken pieces together again.

Discovering Your Voice

Because of my time in God's Word, his voice was breaking through my chaos. I was beginning to understand John 10:3–4:

> The gatekeeper opens the gate for him, and the sheep listen to his **voice**. He calls his own sheep by name and leads them out. When he has brought out all his own, he goes on ahead of them, and his sheep follow him because they know his **voice**.

To find my voice, I needed to recognize Jesus' voice and to follow him as he was leading me.

- Prayerfully consider when, in your life, you have heard Jesus calling you and leading you into new territory. Did you risk following him?
- Think of a time when you used your voice and it did not go over well. How did you respond? How would you want to respond today?
- In what areas should you be using your voice but you feel intimidated? What resources can you use to help you find strength to express that voice? Counseling? Friends? Bible study or small group leaders? Your pastor?

Listen for Jesus' voice. He is telling you that you are precious to him. Take the risk to follow his lead, for he is going out ahead of you, leading the way.

Remember, you are loved! You are *liked!*

CHAPTER TEN

Sanctuary

There I was finding my voice, beginning to use my voice, making some real headway, when I took a wrong turn. A terribly willful, sinful, destructive wrong turn. I have no desire to try to avoid it, excuse it, sugarcoat it, or explain it away.

By 1993 I found myself separated from John and in love with and having an affair with another man, Don Peslis. Not only did I commit adultery, I lied to cover it up. This was painfully revealed in a very public divorce. I've told the story in my book *Broken on the Back Row,* and through it I shared the remarkable impact of God's grace and my journey of restoration through my church. There would be little point in retelling the whole tale here because frankly, it takes an entire book to tell the story. But because *this* book is about listening for God's voice and finding our own voices through the highs and lows of life's journey, I'd be leaving out some critical turning points and awesome breakthroughs if I simply skipped over this season of my life.

Let me interject here that there are always reasons for our behavior, and we must be attentive to and understand those reasons if we are to learn from our mistakes and grow. But *reasons* are never *excuses*—and I make no excuses for my sin. As in previous chapters, I have attempted here to give context for particular situations in my life. Context is given only to help you understand the process and discoveries and is never given for justification. I just want to be really clear on that. I've had a couple of people over the years say to me, "Thank you for your book. I felt like I could get a divorce because you did." Whoa. Whoa. Whoa! That wasn't the point of *Broken on the Back Row* at all. My heart grieved when I heard that. I certainly don't want to risk hearing it again on this book.

What I would like to do is share three milestones in my journey through this time of great brokenness. These milestones stand as markers of three choices I made to use my voice—choices that brought me face to face with God's faithful and grace-filled intervention in my life. I pray they inspire you to place your trust in God and to listen closely for his voice no matter how deep your brokenness, how devastating your sin, or how debilitating your pain. And as you listen for God's voice, hear the call of the Holy Spirit in Hebrews 3:15: "Today, if you hear his voice, do not harden your hearts as you did in the rebellion."

I rebelled against God's standards for a time, and in that rebellion, I hardened my heart against God's voice. I reaped the terrible consequences of my choices and, even more painfully, watched horrified as my children paid the price for my choices as well. I wound up shattered—personally and professionally.

So I appeal to you, as you read, soften your heart and draw near to the God who sees you fully and loves you unconditionally.

Confiding in Mom and Dad

When I realized that my marriage to John was coming to an end, I knew I had to break my silence and confide in my parents. I had been in counseling for a couple of years by then and felt validated and confident enough to share the many things that had gone on in my marriage and were still going on. Of course, I was prepared for them not to agree with or validate my actions. I knew that their love for God, his Word, and his standards was unshakable. This is how I knew they were safe to confide in. I didn't need them to agree with my actions; I only needed them to know the truth.

A side note here. I realize how blessed I am to have parents who are safe people, and I acknowledge that there are many people for whom family is not safe. If that is you, apply this example to a few wise, safe believers who can play this role in your life—and pray for God to reveal to you who they may be.

On my way to their home, I wept, knowing how heartbroken and grieved they would be with my news. As I poured out my heart to them, I didn't try to hide how bitter and angry and hurt and disappointed and shamed and guilty I was. They were grieved, of course, but their unconditional love for me remained unshaken. They listened with empathy as I shared the unhealthy enmeshment of our marriage and business and how two very broken people had created such a broken marriage.

But then Mom surprised me. Now, remember, I thought my parents never had conflicts because I had never witnessed any discord between them. Now, however, my mom shared that oh yes, they did. They had some doozies. They had decided to always handle their conflicts privately away from us kids, but now she described to me how over the years they had faced and resolved conflicts. They shared that at times, marriage was a real challenge. *What?* This was the first time I'd heard anything about this. I almost blurted, "Well, hello. This would have been nice to know before now!" Of course,

I understood their decision as parents to keep this to themselves. I so respect their hearts and motives in not wanting the kids to "always" see them argue. I get that totally. They hadn't wanted their conflicts to worry us. But today, I do think a healthy dose of conflict resolution modeling goes a long way with kids.

Their revelations stunned me. But so many things from the past now made sense. This new knowledge also made me feel not so alone in my struggles. My mom shared she'd had a difficult time finding her voice with my dad, and that process took them a while. My mom's voice might be soft, yet it has become one of the most important voices in my life. Many times since that discussion, I've said to her, "I wish I had known. I wish I had known," because then I wouldn't have been so afraid to share with her. She would have understood and could have been a great source of wisdom and comfort for me before things got so irreparable, before things got to a place where the wounds were just too great and there needed to be an amputation.

Through that encounter with my parents, my mom became, and remains to this day, one of my most trusted confidants. I can tell her anything. And boy, have I! And yet she doesn't flinch. I've told her stuff over the last twenty-five years that I know has unsettled her in difficult ways. But she listens and she champions my voice. I also now understand that my precious dad, whom I've always seen as extremely confident and without a care in the world, chooses always to see the joy in circumstances. He wants to encourage, rather than silence, someone's voice. But I had not realized that prior to that difficult day.

Somehow, in the act of using my voice to share the loss of my marriage and the blatant error of my ways, I gained a far richer, deeper relationship with my parents. And to my surprise, that has also given me a far richer, deeper relationship with God, my heavenly parent. For both Mom and Dad expressed their total and unconditional love and compassion for me. They modeled how God's love can remain unshaken even when we blow it big time and how he is tender when we confess our sins and hand over the broken pieces of our lives. God, just as my parents demonstrated for me, comes alongside and helps us as we pick up the shards and begin to put those jagged pieces together again.

How grateful I am that I used my voice to expose my folly, to share my pain, and to express my needs. I urge you to use your voice to do the same. Find a few safe, godly, experienced confidants. People like my parents. People who don't excuse your sin but still offer you *sanctuary*.

Clinging to the Body of Christ

Even during the chapter of my life when my sin was in full swing, I continued my lifelong custom of attending church. Not only was I committed to providing a church home and a foundation of faith for my four young children, I also never lost sight of the fact that I needed God and his presence and his people. I wasn't fooling myself. I knew that some of my actions were outside of his will. Yes, there was a huge disconnect between my faith and my actions, but that disconnect didn't eradicate my faith. It was struggling, but it was there. Thankfully, the Spirit continued to thrive within me, calling me away from sin, calling me home. And oh, how I longed to be home. I was *so* hungry—even though it was through my own actions that I was starving myself.

Oh, how sin twists and distorts our thinking! Twisted and distorted as I was, every Sunday morning found me in church, and on my weeks to have them, my kids with me.

However, attending the church where John and I had been married was too painful. Besides, I was still trying to portray the image that all was well and that I had it all together, even though my world was falling apart. One Sunday, on a week when I had the kids, I drove us to a different church, North Anderson Church of God. I escorted the kids to their new Sunday school classes, then happened to notice the stairway leading to the balcony. I found myself climbing higher and higher until I finally settled into the very back row. When the service began, I started to cry and cry and cry. Perhaps it was the privacy I'd found on the back row, yet still surrounded by God's people, that released the torrent, but I wept through the entire service—the music, a baby dedication, the sermon. It was a relief to be in a sanctuary without having to wear my fake happy face, so I wept freely.

What happened as the service ended proved to be one of the most remarkable encounters with the voice of God I've ever had in my life. It began as Pastor Jim Lyon stepped down from the pulpit to say a few closing words. I wrote about it in *Broken on the Back Row:*

> "If you're visiting with us today, we're so glad you're here," he said. *Oh please don't make the visitors stand up,* I prayed, trying to find a dry tissue and hoping my mascara had not slid down to my chin.
>
> But the pastor continued, "There are people all around you who would like to know your name if you would like to tell them," he offered. And then he added, "We want you to

know that the God we serve lives within these walls—and outside these walls, too."

He took a few more steps down the aisle and looked all around the crowd. "But maybe you've been visiting with us here this morning, and you're not ready to tell anyone your name. Maybe all you want to do is sit on the back row of the balcony and cry. That's okay," he said. "We want you to know that the God we serve knows how to find you there. He hasn't forgotten about you. We serve the God of second chances, of new beginnings. We serve the God who sets His children free.'"*

The voice of God had spoken. To me. Directly. And God wasn't telling me I'd out-sinned his grace or that I'd forfeited the right to come to worship him. Those words from the pastor made me realize that God was *seeing* me. God was, indeed, hearing my voice, my cries for mercy. I was hearing from God, *Sandi, you are not alone. I see you no matter where you are. I am the God of new beginnings and second chances.* It was truly one of the most impactful moments for me as I began to trust that I was hearing his voice. And his voice was clearly saying, *Come to me.*

It was because of that God encounter that I decided to call the pastor the following week. The baggage I was carrying was getting really heavy—too heavy to carry alone. I shared my voice of shame and pain with him. I remember saying to him, "I don't care what the world finds out. I don't care if I never sing another song or if I never make another album or I never have a song played on the radio or

---

* Sandi Patty, *Broken on the Back Row* (New York: Howard, 2005), 85–86.

I never get to sing at a church again. . . . I just want to be right and clean before my Father."

It wasn't until I surrendered to the pain, the consequences, the truth, the acknowledgment of my sin, the brokenness handed to me by others, and the wounds I was inflicting upon myself and those around me that I was finally ready to get well and invite healing into my life.

When you become willing to open yourself to hear truth, you notice it everywhere. It was God's Word that first opened my heart to truth. And through God's Word, I started to grow. From there, I recognized truth when I heard it.

Speaking the truth about my life didn't make all the pain and poor choices go away. But there is a freedom that comes when we finally speak our truth out loud in our own voice. Secrecy no longer holds us captive to shame. Acknowledging the truth is an important first step toward freedom. Thanks to that first step of confessing to my pastor, I was able to follow a carefully laid-out path, directed by him and the church council, that led me through the process of confession, restoration, and healing. It was not an easy journey. Far from it. But it was worth every second of effort and tears and pain. A church, I discovered, should not only *have* a sanctuary. It should *be* a sanctuary.

Healing in a Safe Place

On the heels of my decision to confess the whole truth to Pastor Lyon came another decision. I realized that I had so much internal work to do that it was far more than could be accomplished once a week in an hour with a counselor. So after much thought and prayer and godly guidance, I decided that I needed to check myself in to a Christian psychiatric ward for two weeks. There God truly created the safest sanctuary for me. There I felt I could be authentic, not some trumped-up version of the famous recording artist Sandi "Patti" (I was still going by the misspelled name) but the real Sandra Faye Patty.

Once I became an inpatient, it took me a while to believe that the staff and my fellow patients wanted to get to know the woman behind the music and songs. For the first few days, I wasn't convinced. I told them, "I'm not going to sing. Don't ask me about my career. Don't ask about Sandi Patti or about tour."

"No problem," my therapist responded. "What else do you need?"

Had I ever been asked that question before? What did I need? At first it was hard to come up with an answer. I finally said, "I need to be able to choose to leave if I want to."

My therapist said, "Go ahead. You can leave anytime you want."

"Oh, right," I challenged. "That door is locked."

"I can unlock it for you anytime you want."

"Then unlock it now."

And she did.

I walked out the door to the elevator, rode down to the ground floor, and walked outside. It had just begun to snow, and everything looked so fresh and new and perfect to me. I stood there for a moment drinking it all in. My therapist, who had followed me, said, "Now what do you need?"

With tears in my eyes, I said, "I guess I need to get back in there and get to work."

"Okay, then," she said. "How about we do just that?" And that is what we did. Once I understood that I truly had the freedom to *choose,* I worked terribly, wonderfully hard. It was uncomfortable to talk about certain things—especially in front of other patients. The work made me sad and angry and anxious. I wept. I punched my pillow. And through it all, I discovered the freedom to express, to say, to feel, to be authentic. It was tremendously healing. I have to say that I found more truth and honesty in those two weeks on that psych ward than I have found in most churches. The stories that poured out of other patients astounded me. And instead of anyone being judged or shamed, they were applauded and congratulated for being brave enough to speak the difficult truth.

As God revealed the broken areas of my life and then restored them, I saw in my story that God had saved all my tears and was now using them to water my soul. Bruised and battered and broken, I found my way into the grace and mercy of my Savior. And it seemed to me that both Jesus and I wept tears of sorrow and regret as well as tears of joy and gratitude.

Whenever a person left the ward, the residents gathered and spoke words of affirmation to them. When it was my time to leave, their affirming words were such sweet gifts to my spirit. Then I said to them, "It has been a long time since I can remember wanting to give a song away, but I'd like to sing for you, if that's okay." And there, in what had become such a tender place, I sang, a cappella, "Take My Hand, Precious Lord."

I have tears in my eyes even as I am writing these words, remembering those powerful feelings. At the time, I thought, *This is what church is meant to feel like. Not a place where you hide your pain but a sanctuary to allow God to do what needs to be done to bring healing.*

Discovering Your Voice

Like me in the balcony that day, you, too, are seen by God. And there is no reason to hide from him, no matter what chapter of your story you may be living. With Jesus, you are safe.

- Who has God placed in your life who might provide you with a safe place to share your brokenness—who might be a sanctuary? A few individuals, a church home, a professional Christian counselor?
- How might you use your voice, now, to reach out for sanctuary?

Hear the voice of Jesus calling out to you in John 7:37:

> On the last and greatest day of the festival, Jesus stood and said in a loud **voice**, "Let anyone who is thirsty come to me and drink."

Did you notice what kind of voice Jesus used there? A *loud* voice! He wanted to make sure he was heard. I pray that you, too, hear his invitation to you to come and drink, for Jesus can quench our thirst to be seen and to be safe.

CHAPTER ELEVEN

The Scarlet A and Other Capital Letters

My dear friend Carolyn is a wise woman. We have been friends for many years. She'd been one of those faithful friends who stood by me when I decided to speak the truth about the sin and mistakes in my life. I wanted to be right and clean before the Lord and was submitting myself under the covering of my church to walk through the biblical restoration process. I had gone to those I needed to go to—including John, and Don's wife, Michelle, to ask forgiveness. I was doing everything I knew to do.

Carolyn (who has since become a licensed professional life coach) and I were talking one day, and I was sharing with her the depth of my feelings of regret and disappointment in myself. "I feel such shame for so many of my choices," I said. "I can't escape the worry and concern for my kids and how I hurt my family."

Carolyn said, "Sandi, you are carrying things that I thought you said had been laid at the cross."

"I know. I know. But I don't for one second take this lightly. I feel the weight of it with me all the time. God has forgiven me for my sin, I know. But sin has consequences, and the consequences of my sins haven't gone away. That doesn't mean I'm not forgiven. I am forgiven and I know it, but look at the price my kids and Don's kids are paying—and will continue to pay. I want to walk in the light and in the truth of forgiveness, but the shame just clings to me."

Carolyn wasn't one to give up. "Come on," she said, "we're going on a field trip. Get in the car."

"Where are we going?"

"You'll see," she said. We took my car, and I followed her directions as I drove. We ended up at Lowe's—of all places—and we walked directly to the garden and patio section. She walked over to the big square cement stones (the kind you make a pathway with) and said, "Okay, pick one."

"Pick one what?" I asked.

"Pick one of these stones. Make sure it's heavy. We're gonna buy it."

I attempted to pick one up, and boy, it was heavy. It was sixteen inches square and weighed about twenty-five pounds. I had no idea what we were going to do with it, but I carried it to the cash register and paid for it. Clearly, Carolyn had something in mind.

The nice young man at the register asked if I needed help getting it to the car, but before I could say, "Why, yes, I do. Thank you very much," Carolyn piped in. "No, we're fine. She can carry it."

So I picked up that slab of cement and began walking to the car. It seemed to get heavier the farther I carried it. When I got to the car, I realized that my keys were in my purse.

Carolyn said, "What's the matter?"

"I've got to put this slab down to get my keys," I said, looking around for a good place to set it on the ground.

"Well, the rules are," she said (and I was thinking, *Rules?*), "you can't put the stone down. You have to carry it with you everywhere you go." So with some shuffling and anchoring my hip on the car door, I finally got my keys out. Now, of course, I had to drive. Fortunately, I learned there was one exception to the rule—I didn't have to drive with the stone. (That just wouldn't be smart.)

When we got back to my place, Carolyn asked, "What do you have to do next?"

"Well, I need to put in some laundry and get dinner started because the kids will be coming home from school soon."

She said, "Okay, here's the deal. Wherever you go and whatever you are doing throughout the day, you have to carry the stone with you."

I looked at her like she was nuts. "I'm supposed to carry this stone with me?"

"Yep."

"You're out of your mind."

"You don't get to comment or ask questions. Just do it."

At first, I thought she was just playfully fooling around. Then I realized that she was quite serious. I was irritated at that point, but my respect for Carolyn outweighed my irritation, and I decided to follow her instructions.

Here are a few things that happened as the day wore on.

Because I was carrying the stone, I couldn't hug the kids very well when they got home from school.

"Mom, what's with the cement?"

"Ask your Auntie Carolyn." Because Carolyn was still there, making sure that I followed her instructions.

It took me so much longer to do the simplest of tasks—like start chili for supper. One arm was always holding the stone, so I had only one hand to work with. Then my arms got tired, and I got mad that I had to carry this stupid stone in the first place. After dinner I had to go to some school meeting, where I was completely and utterly embarrassed that I had to hold my precious stone for everyone to see, but there was no hiding it.

A Slab of Shame

I quickly (as I'm sure you have as well) surmised the point of this little exercise. It's exhausting carrying around our slabs of shame. And tiring and humiliating and frustrating and inconvenient. It's hard to do life when you're constantly having to deal with a giant cement slab.

Finally, later in the evening, Carolyn said, "Why don't you just put it down?"

I wanted to smack her. Now my pride was invested, and I wasn't going to quit holding on to this stupid stone. I had to prove to her (and everyone) that I could hold it, that I could function while I carried it. And then she said again, "Why don't you just put it down?"

Jesus' words in Matthew 11:28–29 came to me with new meaning: "Come to me, all you who are weary and burdened, and I will give you rest. Take my yoke upon you and learn from me, for I am gentle and humble in heart, and you will find rest for your souls." It was as if the Lord was saying to me, *Sandi, why don't you just lay down your shame? Bring it to me. I know how weary you are. I know you are heavy with heartache and shame. You no longer need to carry that burden. Lay it down by giving it to me.*

"Oh, but God," I prayed, "I don't want anyone to think that by letting go of my shame, I am taking my choices lightly. I sinned. I had an affair. I got a divorce. I hurt people. I extinguished relationships. I need to pay. I'm a bad girl. It was all my fault."

Suddenly I heard all of the voices of "me" over the years. The six-year-old girl, the "Fatty Patty," the thick cheerleader, the girl who dumped her date on prom night, the girl who had an affair, the girl who filed for divorce. And then I heard again in my spirit, *Just lay it down. Give it to me.*

A verse came to my heart in that moment: "If we confess our sins, he is faithful and just and will forgive us our sins and purify us from all unrighteousness" (1 John 1:9).

I had confessed my sin. I had gone before my entire church to confess my sin. I had gone individually to people of whom I needed to ask forgiveness. *Lay it down. Just lay it down,* that still, small voice said.

I began to cry. "I want to put it down," I said to Carolyn, "but now I've gotten used to it. I am tired of carrying it, though."

"Then let me help you put it down," she said, and I agreed. And with tears in our eyes, she helped me put down the slab. We just put it down, and I walked away. Well, it wasn't exactly that easy because I had to find a place to discard it. Which is effort in itself. After all, you can't just leave a slab in the hallway of your home. People would start tripping over it. Right? But we found a place to set it somewhere between the laundry room and the kitchen, gently, as if that slab had become an altar of surrender. The next day, I moved it to the back seat of my car, and for many weeks I carried it there as a powerful reminder that my slab of shame was no longer mine to carry but had been left at the foot of the cross.

The Scarlet Alphabet

My slab of shame could have been stamped with *A* for adultery, abuse, and addiction, *D* for divorce, *P* for pride. I could go on. I bet you could choose letters to create your own alphabet slab of shame.

Thank God our lives don't come to a screeching halt when a new letter is etched into our slab. Oh, how I am encouraged that God uses imperfect people! Just look at the cast of characters in the Bible. They messed up—a lot. But those who were willing to lay down their slabs and allow God to forgive and change them, they were the ones who found that God could still use them. They didn't stay stuck in their messes. They laid their messes down. They wept tears of repentance and change and watched as God erased those letters and left an altar in their place, a monument to what God had accomplished in them.

Did many of them still have consequences to live with? Oh yes, the Bible is filled with the consequences of sin, but those who chose obedience went on to accomplish great things for the kingdom of God. Just read the eleventh chapter of Hebrews for a refresher course on the Hall of Faith, but make sure you don't stop there. You must turn the page to read Hebrews 12:1–3, which says, "Therefore, since we are surrounded by such a great cloud of witnesses, let us throw off everything that hinders and the sin that so easily entangles. And let us run with perseverance the race marked out for us, fixing our eyes on Jesus, the pioneer and perfecter of faith. For the joy set before him he endured the cross, scorning its shame, and sat down at the right hand of the throne of God. Consider him who endured such opposition from sinners, so that you will not grow weary and lose heart."

Wow, that was written for me. And for you. We have the great joy set before us of standing with Jesus Christ at the throne of God, face to face, just as the lyrics of "We Shall Behold Him" proclaim.

If you have been where I have been, or maybe, even as you are reading this, you are in the midst of a sinful choice in your life, know that God *adores* you. He wants to wrap his cloak of grace around you just like he did for the woman caught in adultery. Today can be a beginning. For you. Just lay down your sin and shame. Speak the truth, even when that truth is personal and ugly. Where there is truth, there is God. And where there is God, there is freedom.

We all still wear a scarlet letter, but it is one that God has given us. He has taken our scarlet *A*s and *D*s and *P*s and any other letter you can think of, and he has replaced them with his own *A*, for atonement, because that is what he has done for us. Atonement—satisfaction or reparation for a wrong or injustice. Amends. Jesus did that for us. I'll wear his scarlet *A* any day!

Changed for Good

Just so we're clear. I hate divorce. God hates divorce. Anyone who has been through a divorce or walked alongside someone going through a divorce hates divorce. But for me, divorce was my new normal. I couldn't go back and undo what had been done. I had to move on from where I stood. Praise God, though, I didn't have to move on alone.

I walked into my first marriage with so much baggage, I couldn't see clearly. And so did my first husband. We all do. But he and I never acknowledged our baggage, and therefore we never got help to deal with it—not from friends or counselors or pastors. We didn't do any premarriage counseling. Let me just stop right here and address that—if you intend to marry, do your prep work. Look at your baggage. Look at it together. Look at it individually. But look at it. Unpack it. Throw out what you need to. Take the personality tests. Seek to understand how you and your mate relate. Introvert? Extrovert? What is your love language? It's all so important. Your baggage drives and guides you in ways you cannot even see. Take a risk. Talk to a wise Christian friend. Talk to a pastor or counselor. But do the work. You are worth it. Your marriage is worth it.

At the close of my restoration period, in late 1994, I decided to make a change that would signify the restoration and healing that had been taking place inside of me. I officially "corrected the mistake" of the spelling of my last name. I changed my performance name from the mistaken P-a-t-t-i to my real family name, P-a-t-t-y. I found that my voice had grown strong enough to announce to my recording label that I wanted now to be known by my given family name, and they gladly complied. What a joyous outward sign of my internal healing and newfound strength!

After my restoration period, and then after more wise counsel and a significant waiting period, Don Peslis and I were blessed to get married in 1995. (As of this writing, we have been married for nearly twenty-three years.) For some time, because of the public nature of my career, the media continued to be morbidly fascinated with my fall from grace. I tried to play damage control for a good while, but I finally decided, *If the truth is going to come out, I'd rather it came from me.* So with the help of my pastor, my accountability group, and my church, we set aside a Sunday morning to share our story publicly. It wasn't fun. It was hard. But let me tell you, it was also freeing. Because now there was nothing more to be afraid of. I had spoken the truth, unleashed the secrets. Our sharing came with a lot of hard consequences, but I no longer had to carry the load that comes with trying to hide the truth. The truth truly does make you free.

Throughout the few years of this long ordeal, I learned that there are friends who don't know how to walk alongside someone who is hurting. That's okay. I did lose friends along the way. I also learned that there were friends who were aware that my life was about to implode, and they quietly came alongside me and gave me a soft and safe place to fall. And there were friends who helped me, like Carolyn. Some friends were quite unexpected. Perhaps the most unexpected friends were the ones who had traveled a similar path long before I had. They knew what it looks like to be broken and bruised. So they were able to say, "Come on. It's okay. We're here for you. Press on."

I have been reminded over and over of this: We are not alone! There are those who have fought the fight before us. And there will be those who come behind us to whom we can say, "Come on. It's okay. You're safe. You're not alone. I am here for you. Jesus is here with you. Press on."

When I started counseling, my therapist said to me, "Sandi, people come into our lives for a reason, a season, or a lifetime." I have loved that saying because it reminds me that there is a purpose to all of the relationships God places in our lives. It could be only for a season, or it could be for a lifetime, but listen for God's voice at work in the people he brings across your path.

In the Broadway musical *Wicked* is a song called "For Good." The first time I heard it, I was in the car with some of my girls. They were going on and on about this song and how great it is.

"Mom, you have to hear this song," one of my daughters said. So they played it for me. As I listened, I couldn't control my heart. The lyrics, the music, the singers, the message—such a powerful combination. I couldn't even speak I was so moved. Listening to it threw me back to my counseling years. But then it cast my view forward, and I contemplated the beautiful hope of more God-given relationships on the path ahead. The lyrics speak of being changed for the better and being changed *by one another* "for good," with the double entendre of "for good" meaning both "forever" and "for the better." Go online and read the lyrics!

Like the song says, we have the ability to change someone's life, and they have the ability to change ours. I believe that's especially true during the worst times in our lives. I can now look back on some of my most difficult chapters and embrace those seasons as times rich in friendship. The friendships changed me. God changed me. I have been changed "For Good."

Some years ago, I had the opportunity to meet Kristin Chenoweth. She was the original star of *Wicked*. She, along with another character, sang "For Good" in the musical. Kristen is from Oklahoma, and I'm from Oklahoma. Before we met, our paths had crossed via social media and through a mutual friend. I had heard her say in interviews that my music had meant a great deal to her over the years, and at one point she covered one of my songs, "Upon This Rock."

Anyway, to make a short story long (see what I did there?), I had an opportunity to see and hear her in concert with the Indianapolis

Symphony Orchestra a few years ago. She invited me onstage to sing "For Good" with her. And for all of the reasons I have mentioned in this chapter, it was a reminder that God uses others to change us for good.

Discovering Your Voice

I have found that the alphabet can be a handy little tool in our spiritual lives. Consider these alphabet questions:

- What "capital letters" of the alphabet still haunt you from your past?
- Just as I discovered that *A* for atonement is a far more powerful letter in my life than those old letters stamped on my slab of shame, what other wonderful letters has God stamped in your life? Here are just a few to consider: *F* for forgiven, *C* for comforted, *G* for guided, *L* for loved.

You and I have the opportunity to make sure that others who pass through our lives need not face their trials alone. Mysteriously, in ways that only God can fully understand, he can use us to help others change for good. As you contemplate the following verse (Job 37:5), consider how amazing it is that sometimes God uses us to be his voice in the lives of others, and others to be his voice in our lives.

> God's **voice** thunders in marvelous ways;
> he does great things beyond our understanding.

CHAPTER TWELVE

Voice Lessons

The beautiful thing about getting healthy is that you grow in new ways—new behaviors, new boundaries, new words, new friendships. The hard thing about getting healthy is that you grow in all those same ways—new behaviors, new boundaries, new words, new friendships. Learning something new when you have long-established patterns can be a significant challenge. Put another way, growth is just downright hard. Worth it, but hard. That's as true for growing into your new voice as it is for any other kind of change.

I have a friend who is a recovering alcoholic, now five years sober. I recently noticed that he was doing many new things—traveling a good bit and taking some cooking and art classes. I finally asked him why he was so busy and how he could still be working full time yet have so much time to play.

He said, "Sandi, you have to understand that I spent so much time drunk, I had to figure out what to do with all this extra time. I've had to learn how to live differently. Now that I'm sober, I have so much time that I didn't used to have, so my sponsors from Alcoholics Anonymous encouraged me to learn new things."

I believe that those of us who are growing from voicelessness into the full expression of who we are created to be in Christ Jesus would do well to follow my friend's example. Let's invest ourselves in learning new skills to live differently so that our voices become richer and fuller expressions of who we are in Jesus. We must set ourselves up for success. We can make a plan and work our plan to develop and strengthen our voices.

Mom's Practice Sessions

Earlier I wrote about how the precious step of confiding in my parents led to enjoying a newfound relationship with my mother—one of confiding in one another. One day, not too long ago, Mom stunned me with some new information about herself as a young mom. Her story has revolutionized my perspective on how to grow and develop one's voice.

My mom shared that, in her family of origin, she knew that she was loved, but she never really heard the words. Her parents simply were not verbally expressive of their love with one another or with her. Consequently, before her marriage to my dad, she never learned how to say the words "I love you." They simply weren't a part of her vocabulary. When she and my dad got married, my dad was very free to say "I love you." Slowly, my mom learned how to say "I love you" back to him. But when my two younger brothers and I were born, Mom worried that she wouldn't know how to naturally say "I love you" to us.

So Mom, determined to become comfortable and natural in expressing her love verbally, would wait at night until we three were sound asleep. Then she would sneak into our bedrooms and stand over us in the dark and practice saying those important words.

"I love you, Sandi."

"I love you, Mike."

"I love you, Craig."

She practiced saying the words so that when the time came, she would feel comfortable saying them to us. Isn't that a beautiful picture of a young mother eager to grow into using her voice to be the kind of mother she wanted to be?

One reason Mom's story shocked me so much is that, if you knew my mom now, you would never ever know that she once had trouble saying "I love you." She says those words freely to everyone today. Mom is famous among our friends and family for saying those words—for speaking words of love to others. She even takes your face in her hands and makes sure you are looking at her. She looks right in your eyes and says, "You know I love you, right? I love you today."

She started adding *today* several years ago when my youngest brother, Craig, was in a serious car crash. He sustained a head injury and was in a coma for many weeks. There were days we prepared our hearts for his move to heaven. And so, not knowing how much longer we would have him on this earth, and not knowing whether we would have him *tomorrow,* she added the word *today.*

"Craig, I love you *today!*" And so now that has become a family story and a constant saying for all of us. We love you today!

The Mechanics of Voice Lessons

I'd like to follow my mom's example and practice using my voice as a spiritual-growth tool. I'd like to practice using my voice according to the will of God. This makes me think of taking voice lessons.

The Voice

The object of voice lessons is to maximize the proper use of your vocal cords for the greatest possible range, quality, and control of the sounds you produce. You do so by practicing certain vocal phrases, starting with vibrations low and slow, then stretching and strengthening the cords by going from low, to higher, back to low, then higher still, and so on, continually stretching to higher levels with greater and greater control and quality over time. You also must learn to breathe correctly, for breathing is the anchor of a strong, healthy voice.

I was reading Philippians 4:4–9 recently, and it sparked an illustration of how we can grow and practice our spiritual voices. Here is the rich instruction that Paul wrote to the believers in Philippi:

> Rejoice in the Lord always. I will say it again: Rejoice! Let your gentleness be evident to all. The Lord is near. Do not be anxious about anything, but in every situation, by prayer and petition, with thanksgiving, present your requests to God. And the peace of God, which transcends all understanding, will guard your hearts and your minds in Christ Jesus.
>
> Finally, brothers and sisters, whatever is true, whatever is noble, whatever is right, whatever is pure, whatever is lovely, whatever is admirable—if anything is excellent or praiseworthy—think about such things. Whatever you have learned or received or heard from me, or seen in me—put it into practice. And the God of peace will be with you.

The vocal performer in me sees a formula there for training our spiritual voices. Mind you, I realize this is a rather unconventional application of these verses, but stay with me and see if it rings as true for you as it does for me.

Start with the basic of rejoicing and practice that. This is the "low and slow" equivalent to voice lessons. Next, begin stretching your spiritual voice by making requests of God, with thanksgiving. This takes us to the next higher level and grounds us in peace. Then stretch to the next level by meditating on and saying whatever is true, noble, right, pure, lovely, admirable, excellent, and praiseworthy. Finally, practice, practice, practice.

What if you and I practiced using our voices in these ways? Imagine how beautiful and strong our voices could become.

As the mom of a large blended family, I'd love to influence my family (and friends) by having my voice be one of rejoicing, praying for requests with thanksgiving, abiding in peace, and reflecting on such a wondrous list of qualities, such as whatever is true, noble, right, pure, lovely, admirable, excellent, and praiseworthy, and practicing those habits repeatedly. You see? I'm following in my mother's footsteps of practicing what I want to come naturally to me. Because honestly, this will take a ton of practice! My voice does not naturally follow that path, but how I would love it to!

A New Family

Don and I married in 1995 and were privileged to take two broken families (broken by our sin and shame) and grow them into one vibrant, blended family. This was surely a God-sized task! When we married, I had my four children (Anna, 11; Jonathan, 8; Jenn, 8; and Erin, 5), and Don had three (Donnie, 7; Aly, 6; and Mollie, 3). And six months later, we adopted our son, Sam, who was four days old. It was no small task to transform two adults and eight children into one blended family unit. (I wrote about that process in my book *Life in the Blender.*) That was nearly twenty-three years ago, and we see God's fingerprints all over our family, not because of what we did right but because of what we learned through all of our mistakes. And because God was faithful in answering our many prayers for our family.

Beginning to mother our blended family was like a fresh beginning to parenting, and it was a relief to be able to draw on lessons learned before that fresh start. For instance, one thing I had to learn when I was a brand-new mom is that my kids had needs, and it was okay that they had needs. But I was still in an unhealthy place with unhealthy expectations, and I remember thinking when I was pregnant with my first child, Anna, "I am going to be the best mom ever. My child will never have to cry, because I will anticipate and meet every one of her needs." Seriously? Can you even imagine? The moment Anna was born—and cried—I was a failure.

It really didn't occur to me how unhealthy my expectations were until another more experienced mom said to me, "Sandi, it's so important that your kids express when they need something. It's okay when they cry. If they cry and then someone comes to meet their needs in a healthy way, they learn to trust." Wow. This was a big lesson for me as a new mom. She was telling me that it is important for children to learn to use their voices. When they are little, it's only crying. But as they get older, they form words, and in a natural way, you are teaching them that their voices have value and they are heard.

One priority Don and I had was to encourage each of our kids to develop their voices. We taught and modeled that it is healthy to express positive and negative emotions, to work through conflict and look for a positive outcome, and to express love and affirmation as well as needs and desires. While we were far from being perfect parents, today when we look at our family of young adult children, we are so proud of how each of them uses his or her voice in healthy ways.

To contrast that for just one moment, I've had the opportunity to travel overseas and be hands-on with people who don't have access to necessities like we do in the United States, things like clean water, education, food, and medicine. One thing that has haunted me ever since my first visit to a developing country is that the babies didn't cry. The silence was deafening. They had learned early on that their needs would not be met. And so they simply stopped trying to express their feelings. What a contrast and what a powerful object lesson in encouraging our kids to use their voices to express their needs!

Present Your Requests to God

Practicing the instructions in Philippians about making our requests known to God has had an unanticipated effect on my life. As I've explained, ever since the sexual abuse I suffered at the age of six, I have experienced a strong link between my voice and food. What I am about to share is an area where I am still very much in process, but I share it here because it, too, is an enlightening example of how we grow.

I have a friend who has been going through some monumental challenges in the past couple of years. About a year ago, I felt a call to intercede for him regularly. Devoted intercession was a new spiritual practice for me. I had never really devotedly interceded in prayer before, and I didn't quite know how. I knew I could study about intercession and that God works through prayer to change circumstances, situations, and human hearts. I also knew that God uses prayer to change the one praying, but I never anticipated how he might do so.

Anyway, I began to pray for this person. Some days I didn't even know where he was or whether he was alive. But something would come to my mind and I would pray. I prayed that God would surround this person even right in the moment and give him a little glimpse of God's peace and presence. Then my prayers got bolder, and I prayed that God would break any strongholds the enemy had over this person, that he would see through the lies of the enemy and really believe that he was a worthy and loved child of the King of Kings. I would say to God, "Let him see your truth. Your truth never changes. Let him stop fighting against it and going around it and just step into your truth."

Then the strangest, most wondrous thing happened in me. God took that little phrase, "just step into your truth," and began to work on *me*. Here's the thing I realized: There are truths in the universe that just are. God's truths are the same yesterday, today, and forever. The truth of gravity—it's always the same. The truth of the theory of relativity (which I do not at all understand, but I know it explains certain phenomena in physics) never changes. It will not change no matter how much we might want it to change.

Then this little annoying word popped into my head—calories. *Calories? Where did that come from?* And then I had an internal dialogue about a simple universal truth about calories. If you take in more calories than you burn, you will gain weight. That's it. That's all there is. This principle is not going to change. And no matter how many times over the years I have genuinely and quite creatively tried to wiggle my way around that truth, it doesn't budge. It is simply true.

Frankly, I'm still working on this one. It's a big one for me. But the point that became crystal clear to me is this: How can I pray down strongholds in someone else's life if I'm not willing to pray them down in my own? So if I want to lose weight and get an understanding of the role food plays in my life, I have to abide by God's rules. These rules aren't meant for my misery. They are meant for my freedom. So now I am submitting, and I gladly give this struggle to my heavenly Father. Jesus said he has come to give us life and life abundant. This means he wants us to enjoy the life he has given us.

So given that principle of calories, I need to learn new practices. Instead of grabbing food, which has always been my "go to," I have to learn what to do and what not to do. I have so many more options than just grabbing whatever food is handy. For instance, I can decide not to leave chocolate chip cookies around, and not to keep unhealthy snack foods I really like in the cupboard. My recovering alcoholic friend, the one I spoke of at the beginning of this chapter, doesn't leave alcohol around because that was his "go to" in times of stress or need for comfort. I need to exercise that same wise choice with snack foods. Just don't do it.

That's where I am today. A work in progress. Putting into practice what I've learned from Philippians, I am rejoicing that God is all powerful and can break through my strongholds. I am making my request known to God: *Lord, break through this area in my life where the enemy has such a hold on me. Help me to step into the basic truth that if I take in more calories than I burn, I will gain weight.* And I'm offering thanksgiving to God that he hears my voice and knows my struggle and looks on me with compassion. I am also praying for his peace in this area, and I am choosing to think on what God has shown me to be true, noble, right, pure, lovely, admirable, excellent, and praiseworthy when it comes to food. I am learning to trust more and more that God wants what is best for me and to be willing to practice and practice, just like my mom did, so that I may more and more become the person God created me to be.

Discovering Your Voice

Jesus, our Good Shepherd, uses his voice, through the Holy Spirit, to guide us in the way that we should go. As John 10:27 says:

> My sheep listen to my **voice**; I know them, and they follow me.

- What basic truth has Jesus been trying to speak to you? If you don't know, ask the Holy Spirit to guide you to that issue, then guide you in the way you should go from there.
- Are there others whose voices you feel called to encourage or nurture? Who are they? How will you use your voice in their lives?
- What concerns are nudging you to action at this point in your life? How can you use the Philippians model to respond to those needs?

May you experience the peace of God as you rejoice, make your requests known to God with thanksgiving, and think on whatever is true, noble, right, pure, lovely, admirable, excellent, and praiseworthy. Follow Jesus, and practice, practice, practice!

CHAPTER THIRTEEN

Welcome Home

Around 1995—the same year that Don and I got married—I heard about a women's conference that was sweeping the country. It packed out churches everywhere and grew so large it had to be moved to arenas to accommodate all the women who wanted to attend. Thousands of women were drawn to this conference where amazing Christian women talked boldly about real-life stuff—about losing children, depression, abuse, addiction—yet didn't offer platitudes or "one size fixes all" Scriptures.

However, they didn't just talk about the tough stuff. They shared how God had been so faithful and loving in the midst of the painful, broken seasons in their lives. They spoke about finding God not *after* the storm but in the *midst* of it. I think it was Sheila Walsh who said, "Sometimes God will choose to calm the storm. But sometimes, the storm will rage on, and God chooses to calm his child." They shared how he had shown up for them in his Word, relationships, a song, a sweet unexpected gift, or powerful words from someone.

Like so many others, I was drawn to these women because I had always wished that the church could be more open about life's realities. You have to understand, this was new talk. Not many Christians, especially women in the church, had been talking about life and how hard it is. And rarely was anyone talking about how even though the greatest joy in the lives of many women is being a mom, it's also the greatest source of frustration. The underlying impression we got from so many messages around us seemed to be that life as a Christian, especially a Christian mom, is a series of sweet Hallmark movies. The reality is that life is so *daily*. And daily is *hard*. And when you make poor choices (and you will!), it becomes even harder.

Women *loved* coming to what would soon be called the Women of Faith events. The audience would hear these gritty, unpretty stories and think, "Wow, I thought I was the only one to feel this way." It didn't take long for them to realize, "I am not alone. I can talk about my struggles." Just knowing that simple truth helps banish the loneliness and isolation and brings so much hope.

As the Women of Faith events grew, Don and I were at home, working hard adjusting to our new daily normal with our blended family.

One day, while browning hamburger for dinner, I remember telling the Lord, "Oh, God. I know this could never happen because—well, you know, God, the whole divorce thing—but, well, I would love to be a part of the Women of Faith conference. I think my story could help someone else know that they aren't alone." I put my words out there and went on with my daily life, keeping my fragile wish tucked away.

I wasn't really working all that much, which in a way was good because I loved being home, and it felt really important to be there during the early years "in the blender," as we called our blended family. We were learning a lot about ourselves and about each other, and we needed a lot of together time to do that.

I no longer had a manager, and that was okay with me. Because I was rarely being invited to sing anymore, I didn't feel that I needed a manager like I had in the past. But I felt a need for some perspective on my potential for the future. I thought of Mike Atkins. Early in my career, Mike was the concert promoter for many of my first arena shows. He had since retired from concert promotion and was now managing artists full time. On a whim, I took a risk and called him with my big question. "Mike, we haven't had a lot of conversations over the years. But when we have, I know that you've always shot straight with me. So I'm gonna ask you a question and I need you to be bluntly honest." I paused, gathering the courage to ask. "Is my career done? Do I need to just move on to something else?"

It was quiet on his end of the phone for a minute. Then, after taking a deep breath, he said, "Sandi, you asked for my opinion, and I'm going to give it to you straight. I think that, if you want to, the best years of work are ahead of you. You've got a story to tell, if you're willing to tell it. And people need to hear the hope in your story. You've asked me to be honest and I am. You are not finished. You are not done. And if you decide you want to think about working with a new manager, it would be my honor to work with you."

Now the phone was quiet on my end. I hadn't expected that. I had expected him to confirm what I thought I already knew. I could have gone with that assumption and kept silent, never picking up the phone. But by that time, I had learned about using my voice to ask questions—even hard ones. To seek wise and godly counsel. You have to use your voice to do that, no matter how difficult. I had been brave and bold and used my voice to call Mike.

At the time, I didn't realize that using my voice with Mike would change my life.

Time to Dream

Mike came to Indiana the next week to meet with Don and me for dinner. After catching up, Mike said, "I want you two to dream. What would a wish list look like if you could do anything you wanted, Sandi?"

I didn't even have to think about it. I pushed my salad aside and leaned forward. "I've been watching what's happening at the Women of Faith conferences. Mike, the women speakers are so real and honest and genuine. They're not wearing the masks I usually see on women in churches. I love how the audience responds with such relief that they are not alone in their struggles. I think it would be so cool to be part of something so genuine and real. That is my biggest dream." I sat back and placed my used napkin next to my plate and quickly added, before he could deflate the idea, "But I know that won't ever happen because of, you know, the big D and stuff."

He gave a nod and quietly wrote it down on the little napkin we were using for the list.

The years came and went and Mike brought a lot of bookings my way. Appearances I honestly wasn't sure I'd ever do again. Because, you see, on their own, bookings had vanished. Many churches had uninvited me. Bookstores had returned my products. Radio stations no longer played my music. The church at large that had been home since I was born was no longer home. I understood those consequences, but they still hurt. So I was grateful for each booking Mike found me.

During that time, Don and I celebrated our tenth anniversary and the kids were doing well. We had all nestled into this new normal of a blended family.

Then one day Mike called and said, "I've been working on something, and I'd like your blessing to move forward with it."

"Okay . . . spit it out," I said with curiosity in my voice.

He said, "Women of Faith has called . . ."

Audible gasp.

"They want to know if you would join them for their national conference being held in San Antonio next year."

Crickets . . . crickets . . . crickets . . . (That's what you say in the entertainment business when an audience should be responding but they aren't. It's so quiet, you can hear crickets.)

Mike said, "Hey, did I lose you? Are you there?"

"Um . . . *Yes!* Yes, oh my word, of course! Yes. Seriously? Are you joking? Is this for real? Wait . . . for real? Duh times a million! *Yes!*" came my mellow, professional response.

Mike hadn't even told me what they wanted me to do, but I didn't care what it was. I was all in. Just to have the opportunity to be with these women who had spoken into my life—even though they didn't know it. Women I had admired for so long.

Mike said, "Okay, then. I'll continue the conversation with them and see what they would like for you to do and let you know."

Although for the rest of the phone call Mike and I talked mostly business, we both knew that only God could open a door like this one. Only God.

When I hung up, I thought about how years ago I had used my

voice to express my heart's desire out loud—first to God and then to Mike. What if I hadn't? At that moment, I was glad that I was beginning to find, understand, and express my voice. And even better, expressing my own voice was leading me to expect to hear God's voice in return! This was a treasure I wouldn't trade for anything.

A Dream Come True

Early in 2005, the weekend came for me to be a guest in San Antonio. My heart was like the most absorbent sponge ever. I took it *all* in. I wrote notes. Underlined Scripture. Listened to how the speakers crafted and delivered their messages. Just like my years with the Gaithers, I felt I was in a master class, learning how to do life and also how to share my message with others. These women were the best of the best.

After all this richness came my turn to share some songs. A standard part of the Women of Faith program was little mini-concerts throughout the weekend. When it was my turn, just before going onstage, I was standing there thinking, *God, you are really something. You did this. Thank you.*

You have to understand. The stage was not your standard stage with curtained boundaries or backstage where you could hide your backside or feel safe. No, they set this platform in the middle of the arena—a stage in the round. The entire program was out in the open, just like the women who spoke—totally exposed. Vulnerable. No hiding. (How's that for a metaphor for the openness in these events?) The WOF team sat on a little side stage called "the porch," and thus the women sitting there were dubbed the "porch pals."

That night I waited quietly at the bottom of the stairs leading to the platform, my heart racing, my palms sweating, and then . . . I heard my name and off I went.

I can't remember which songs I sang—except for two. And I remember these because Mary Graham, who was the director and emcee for WOF for years, personally requested them. So I closed my mini-concert with "Via Dolorosa" and "We Shall Behold Him."

Honestly, I have to admit there was more going on inside. I was so honored that Mary Graham had called and personally invited me to be part of WOF. But in my head, this is how I assumed it would play out: Mary and the team would be so sweet to me and say stuff like, "We are so glad you could be with us." Then sometime in the next week or so, the WOF office would get letters saying, "I can't believe you had Sandi Patty. Don't you know what a mess she's made of her life?" And so (again this is all in my head) Mary wouldn't want to, but she would call Mike and say, "We loved having Sandi, but we're going to have to uninvite her to any future conferences because we've gotten too many complaints." And Mike and I would say, "We understand, Mary. Just please know what an honor it was for me to be able to be with you all even for that one weekend." I'd have a good cry, and then life would be back to the blessed, ordinary daily.

But that call never came. And I'm thinking, *Just give it more time.* Yet even with more time, the call never came.

One of their artists had suddenly gotten very ill, so they asked me to come to Fort Lauderdale to fill in for her. I agreed. But when my time came, I was quite uncharacteristically scared out of my wits to get up there and sing. It was so important to me to make them proud. I wanted to do well. I wanted to fit in with these awesome women, but in all honesty, it seemed too good to be true. I couldn't shake the feeling that I wasn't worthy to be there, and I still feared that they would soon uninvite me. So much anxiety. Yet what was I to do other than take the stage and sing my heart out? And so I did.

Before the final note of the final song faded, the audience exploded.

I stepped down from the stage and the porch ladies wrapped their arms around me and hugged me so tight and fierce. Chonda Pierce and Kathy Troccoli, who were also guests, came rushing over to me to join the celebration. Chonda said, "Are you hearing this audience, Sandi? Do you *hear* them?" We giggled and jumped and cried and laughed together because they had lived some of that hard season with me. They were celebrating this "homecoming" with me.

The clapping and screaming went on and on as Mary Graham let the audience have their crazy reaction moment. Once the audience had calmed down, Mary looked me square in the eye and said, "Sandi . . . look around. Welcome home."

I couldn't believe it. The people I thought would reject me were celebrating the love of Jesus and the healing and restoration in my life. The sweetness of it all washed over me.

They soon called and asked if I would be willing to fill in permanently for the artist I had replaced. She had had to cancel her appearances at all the remaining conferences for the year.

Wait, they called to *invite* me? Not uninvite me? I couldn't believe it. (Yeah, even after that great crowd reaction, I still thought they might change their minds.) Being part of this event meant I got to sit under the teaching of these amazing women nearly *every* weekend. Are you kidding me?

All of this was very cool, but I still kept my distance because I was *still* so sure they were going to uninvite me. (Such wounds can go deep and take a long time to heal.) I was not going to invest (again, my reality in my head) in these relationships only to get to "that point" where they had so many complaints that they were forced to uninvite me.

Each arena provided a dressing room for me, where I hermited quite a bit. The conference host gave me the option to ride in her car back and forth between the hotel and the venue, or to go on the staff bus. For several weeks, I chose the car, preferring to be by myself. I was truly so afraid that I was going to get hurt that I fiercely guarded and protected myself. The speaker team tried to interact with me and ask questions, but I responded only with standard answers. As I look back on it now, I can see they were allowing me to choose to enter when I felt ready. They weren't going to push or demand. They invited me to share my voice—gently—allowing me the opportunity to choose. They were modeling for me how to honor someone else's voice. Never pressuring my voice to be like theirs. Always waiting for my voice to express itself when it chose. What a gift!

Of course, they graciously asked questions about my husband and family, but I almost fainted when they said, "You need to bring them to a conference."

Wait, what? This crazy, broken, bruised blendedness—you want *all* of us to come?

"Yes," they said. They continued to say it so much that I actually dared to believe their words were true and they meant it. They genuinely were seeking to *see* me. All of me.

One weekend I decided to ditch my driver and ride the bus with the girls. It was like graduating from the kids' table to the grownups' table. I chose to be part of the spontaneous conversations that happened because we were in community. I chose to give an honest answer when someone asked, "How was your week?" I chose to invest in them by asking questions about what mattered to them.

While I was home during the week, all Don heard about were these women. Poor guy. I talked nonstop about how much they meant to me. And he could tell. He could also see that I was growing as a woman. I seemed a little more grounded during the week, not quite so "mom crazy." I was a little bit kinder and more patient.

I was eager for him to meet these new friends, and for them to meet him, so I invited him to come the weekend Women of Faith was to appear in Hartford, Connecticut.

Chonda Pierce was a guest that weekend as well, and during one of the breaks, she said to Mary Graham, "You need to have Sandi and Don sing 'The Prayer.' It's so beautiful."

It's still surprising to me that Mary Graham, who in my opinion is one of the most excellent program producers out there, said yes. She had never heard us sing together, but she trusted Chonda, and I like to think that Mary had learned to trust me as well. So maybe that's the reason she said, "Okay, how about at the end of the next segment?"

When the time came, Mary introduced me and announced that my husband, Don, would be joining me. Luci Swindoll told me later that she had her head in her hands and was praying, "Oh God, please don't let him stink. He's singing with Sandi Patty, for heaven's sake." Hilarious.

The song started and I sang the first verse by myself. Then Don came in on the second verse, singing in Italian, and the ladies swooned. Really . . . there's no other way to say it. Anyway, as the song continued, Luci's head came up little by little. Then she started her Luci giggle, which she does when she really likes something. Then she started wagging her finger at Don like saying "shut up"—in a good way. Before we finished the song, the porch ladies, along with the seventeen thousand ladies in the arena, were on their feet whooping and hollering. As Don and I walked off the stage, the porch ladies were beside themselves. They pretty much grabbed him and said, "We're keeping you." They were laughing and crying at the same time—like you do when something is so touching you just don't have adequate words.

For a moment, I stood outside the situation looking in, completely amazed. Here I had been sure the organizers were going to uninvite me. Now it was clear they not only accepted me but basically had fallen instantly in love with my husband and invited him into the fold. I just couldn't believe it. God's "welcome home" was extended not only to me but to Don as well.

Discovering Your Voice

One of the great joys of being part of Women of Faith is that not only did the women on the platform encourage me but I became part of a team that encouraged the entire audience. Being part of the body of Christ—giving and receiving—is an important element in our spiritual growth.

- How might you use your voice within the body of Christ to encourage others and glorify God?
- If the women in your church or your life seem to be holding back the truth of their lives, how can you model authenticity for them? Ask God to show you what steps you can take to help the women in your church become a true community.
- Think of times in your life when you have heard God's voice better because you expressed your own.

Look at the tremendous role God has for us to play, as revealed in Romans 15:5–6:

> May the God who gives endurance and encouragement give you the same attitude of mind toward each other that Christ Jesus had, so that with one mind and one **voice** you may glorify the God and Father of our Lord, Jesus Christ.

CHAPTER FOURTEEN

Worth the Change

Over the next several years, I continued to be part of the Women of Faith conferences. Every weekend when I walked into those arenas, I never once took that privilege for granted. Never!

Like Don, my family couldn't help but hear the glowing things I was saying about these women. They'd finally heard enough and decided they had to see for themselves and started coming with me. Everyone who was part of this conference loved on our kids and invited them into the circle of grace. And by the way, we needed all the grace we could get!

Blending our family life had been difficult and continued to be busy, let me tell you. Dance, sports, show choir, homework, church. Each week, from the earliest days of being a new family, we would get a big poster board and map out our family schedule, listing each of the kids' activities. It took a lot of coordination to move eight kids plus two adults through life. It was kind of like trying to move a semi-truck on square wheels. It can happen, but it really takes a lot of effort. I'm not gonna lie, the first few years were bumpy. It took us a while to figure stuff out. Thankfully, as the years passed, we adjusted to our blended family. Especially during the Women of Faith years, our kids began to feel a strong sibling connection with each other. Many adults comment to us today that they have never seen siblings be so supportive of each other. Don and I just look at each other and say, "Thank God. We can assure you we had very little to do with that. We had a big 'village.'"

We learned to accept our family. We even encouraged other people who found themselves in similar situations. I believe that we learned to celebrate our family once we were invited into the wonderful safety of the grace exemplified by Women of Faith. Each year, as those women poured into our family and pointed out ways that we were an encouragement to others, we started to believe it. We started to believe that in the story of our brokenness, God was fashioning something new.

Our family now says that Women of Faith loved us back to *life*. Before Women of Faith, of course we loved our family. But I think we focused on the brokenness, weighing us down with unspoken sorrow. Women of Faith saw the beauty in all our brokenness, and because of that, we saw and celebrated the beauty as well. They not only saw God's redemption in our family, they also wanted to rejoice in us—with all the bruises and battered scars. So in 2016, my last year with Women of Faith, my family regularly performed at the mini-concert with me, and oh, what a joy it was to sing with my kids and my husband!

We closed our set with an a cappella arrangement of "It Is Well with My Soul." This particular arrangement had all this lush harmony, and in some places, it had five parts. Because the stage was in the round, the audience was everywhere we looked. We didn't have to face just one side or the other. So on this last song, we decided to stand in a circle and face inward to sing it, first to God but also to each other. We didn't miss the meaning of the words when we sang, "Whatever my lot, thou hast taught me to say, it is well. It is well, with my soul." We knew what we were telling each other—our family was born of loss. And we have endured some tough seasons. But we could now say, some eighteen years later, it *is* well. Whatever the lot. God has *taught* us (I love the word *taught* because it means time and energy were invested in learning something new) to say it is well. It is well, indeed.

What an amazing privilege to be able to sing this truth together.

Through the Women of Faith mini-concerts, we began to celebrate what God was doing and was going to continue to do in our family and in ourselves. As time went along, we were able to step into that celebration with less and less embarrassment and regret. As we talked to those who had come to the conference, we saw that our broken family was an encouragement to others. Maybe we were a bit farther along in our journey, and our progress toward healing offered a bit of hope. Wow! Yes, there are parts of our story we wish we could change. But the truth is the truth, and God can always turn ashes into beauty. He can *always* make things new. We just have to let God do his God thing. And bring to him all of our broken pieces.

It had been eleven years earlier, 2005, when I sang for the first time at Women of Faith. At that time, I think I felt how the woman caught in adultery must have felt. Jesus was her champion. He stood between her and her accusers. I imagine her hiding in his shadow, head bent toward the ground, bracing herself, knowing that in a few moments, she would have to face her accusers with rocks in their hands. But I like to think that when the time came, Jesus actually had to say, "Lift your head. Woman, look around. Where are your accusers?" She barely lifted her eyes to see that, to her astonishment, they were gone. She was expecting to be stoned to death, and now she was safe.

I expected my "stoning" to come in the form of being uninvited from these events. But we both, Don and I, dared to lift our downcast eyes to see Jesus—only Jesus—standing by our side. This is what Women of Faith did for our family. "Come out, come out, wherever you are . . . and be loved and safe."

Balancing the Scales

From then on, I had a little better vision of how God loves, yes, me, too. And I could hear God's voice of love for me through these women. As I traveled with them, I grew so much because I saw them share about their hard times and how God loved them and had been faithful to them in everything, and I more fully believed that Jesus loves me, too. Then, thanks largely to being mentored by the WOF women, during those years I made some life-changing decisions.

Much of my life, I have pictured one of those old justice-type scales in my mind. I would throw all the negative words I used to describe myself onto one side of that scale, and they far outweighed the few positive words I'd hesitantly place on the other. Several things happened through my WOF experience that helped me embrace a larger dictionary of words to describe myself and really tipped the scale the other way for me.

The first decision that I really leaned into was believing that my husband, Don, really does love me and truly thinks I'm beautiful. Don and I have been married now for nearly twenty-three years.

He has always told me how beautiful I am. To be honest, for a long time I didn't believe him. I thought he was just doing the godly husband thing and affirming me as his wife.

Well, then I started to believe that *he* thought it was true. He was so sweet. He would say, "Honey, you are such a beautiful woman. You're kind and funny. You're so attractive."

So, I thought, God must have given him special eyes. But he said these things so much that I started to believe I was beautiful. Maybe I was lovely. Maybe I was pretty. And smart. And funny. I let little pieces of his words slip through those cracks in my skin-armor, and I started acting like I was beautiful and lovely and pretty and smart. Like I mattered.

One day Don asked me a funny question. He said, "Do you think I have poor taste in women? I have good taste in women, and you are my woman."

I decided to take a chance and believe my husband when he said I was pretty. This was a game changer for me.

Over the years of hearing many women's stories of the power of God's redemption in every area of our lives, a truth took root and grew within me, something I'd never believed about myself. These women, through their lives, their words, and their faith, taught me that I am *worth* the effort of making changes in my life.

Let's back up for a moment, because that new belief comes through a several-step process.

If you don't like your behavior in one area or another, in order for new behavior to exist, you have to acknowledge that you *need* to make changes. How many times do we hope the changes will magically happen? They won't. We need to realize that it's up to us (oftentimes with help) to make them. But to change, we also have to acknowledge our *needs* and not feel embarrassed or selfish to use our voices to express those needs. (Remember my *need* to make a choice when I was in the psych ward?) Seeing and acknowledging our needs is a new skill for many of us. It's important for us to acknowledge they are real and honest and truthful—and *okay*.

Once we want to change and can express our needs, then we must come to the understanding that we are worth the effort it will take (and it can take a lot!) to make those changes. Now wait. Don't think this is easy! It's hard to learn something new. After all, you first have to unlearn a whole bunch of stuff. And then, where the old stuff used to be, you have to fill it up with new things. Healthy things. Productive and life-giving things. And that takes time. And effort. Lots and lots of effort. But the changes are worth it.

And I still had a doozy of a change I needed to make.

Oh, Food!

Oh, food! How I love you. Oh, food! How I loathe you.

As a performing artist, I spent much time on the road. And when you spend a lot of time on the road, you spend a lot of time in hotels. And where there's a hotel, there's room service. From which I ordered . . . a lot. It is, after all, convenient—and private—after an exhausting day traveling and performing. Much easier than finding a restaurant. And look at those yummy choices! All that food service was providing more padding than I needed—or wanted.

One year I was at my annual female appointment, and it did not go well. All of my numbers (cholesterol, blood pressure, etc.) were off the charts—and not in a good way. My weight was higher than it had ever been. My sweet doctor friend looked at me and said, "Sandi, what are we doing here? You're killing yourself." She closed her laptop and said, "Have you ever thought about talking to a bariatric specialist?"

"Oh no," I said, smoothing out my fashionable paper gown. "That feels like cheating."

She looked at me with intensity and said, "Sandi, if you don't do something, and do something now, you will cheat your family by dying too soon."

Whoa! That got my attention.

Over the course of the next several months, I made appointments with specialists to see what a bariatric intervention might look like. As I looked carefully at it, it seemed like a really good option for me. The thing is, bariatric surgery isn't cheating. It doesn't make losing weight magic. It just makes it possible. And I wanted possible. I desperately needed possible.

After I decided to take the next step, the only thing I needed was to hear from our insurance company to see if they would cover it. Since insurance didn't always cover this surgery, I was hoping mine would cover just half, deciding that would be my clear sign that I should move ahead with surgery. When the nurse called me, she said, "Sandi, you're not going to believe this. The insurance is covering 100 percent." Wow and wow! We set the date, and I was excited.

I had the surgery. And it wasn't magic. I still must work on the weight issue. But I am so grateful for it. It has been a helpful tool. It was difficult, but I was worth it.

As a result of those two things, along with many others, my dictionary has gotten so much bigger. When a negative defining word comes and wants to tip the scale in my spirit, I have instead God's

Word, my husband's words, my family's words, my church's words, the words from the years in WOF, and I load up the positive side of the scale as though to say, "Here, take that!" And I stand on those words. I stand tall and proud.

As I was writing this book, one of our daughters, Aly, got married. This was a day she had dreamed of her whole life. It was a gorgeous, flawless day, and even the weather cooperated. The wedding took place at a historic plantation just outside of Nashville, Tennessee.

As we gathered for the rehearsal, I realized we were in a place that used to be remembered for the pain and suffering that had occurred there. This was a Confederate graveyard. Even though the plantation had been a safe haven for Union soldiers, it held much pain and sorrow for the Confederate army. We were standing on the place of ultimate sibling rivalry.

But today, there stands an exquisite garden filled with color and life and love. And on those very grounds, many couples pledge their love to one another. This place has been transformed into something new. It now celebrates life where once it was looked upon as a place of death.

As I walked those beautiful grounds, I thought about how the story of the Civil War will never change. It is part of our history as the United States. I know that as Americans, we have parts of our story we wish weren't there. There are stories within our history we wish we could rewrite because they are shameful and embarrassing. Our family has felt all of these feelings. And yet here we were, as we gathered to celebrate Aly and her new husband, Will, at a place that, even though the beginning of its story was filled with pain, had been reshaped and repurposed to celebrate life and love.

That's what God does. God reshapes and repurposes. He brings change. That's God's job, and we just need to get out of the way and let him do what he does. So why stifle our voices and withhold the truth of our broken pieces? He wants us to bring them to him and speak them. He makes all things new.

Discovering Your Voice

You *are* worth the effort it takes to change! Use these questions to nudge you forward:

- In what areas do you hear God, in his love, calling you to change?
- What are the *needs* you've been embarrassed to express—even to yourself?
- What are some changes that God has made in your life that you can celebrate?

Psalm 47:1 (NKJV) is a call to celebrate the changes God has made already and will make in the future.

> Oh, clap your hands, all you peoples!
> Shout to God with the **voice** of triumph!

CHAPTER FIFTEEN

Who Moved the Nest?

Raising eight kids had been . . . well . . . constant. Ha! You thought I was going to say hard or long or busy, didn't you? Well, those words describe it, too, as well as joyous, rewarding, and satisfying. Let's be honest. Childrearing is a complex endeavor—and eight kids in a blended family (remember, all eight were under twelve when we blended) was an endeavor of gigantic proportions. There were many times when we didn't know whether we were coming or going, probably because each of us was always doing one or the other multiple times a day, and often in opposite directions.

But as is the natural order of things, by late 2008, one by one, the oldest six kids had left the nest. One had married, a couple had moved away or were planning to move, and several were in college. Life at home had slowed down considerably, and at this stage of our lives, that felt awesome. I was regularly performing at Women of Faith events, and Don and I found ourselves drawn more and more to a simpler life. We were living a new normal.

Enter a major exciting surprise: Don received a job offer as the director of community outreach for a thriving oil and gas company in Oklahoma City. He lit up at the opportunity, and my heart immediately said yes. It would mean a move from Indiana, where we'd lived since marrying, but a verse from the book of Ruth sprang to mind: "Whither thou goest, I will go; and where thou lodgest, I will lodge" (Ruth 1:16 KJV). I was ready to pack. But first, of course, we needed to discuss it with our two kids who were still living at home. They, too, seemed excited for a new adventure. Since we didn't see the six older kids as frequently as in the past, we assumed that our adult children didn't need us as much anymore. In a lot of ways, it seemed the perfect time for a move.

As we made our plans, however, we noticed that the two kids still at home were feeling hesitant about moving. Don and I talked about various possibilities and were able to present an option for the older of the two to stay in Indiana to finish the last half of her junior year in high school and possibly her senior year as well. So Don and I, along with our youngest, Sam, followed by our daughter, Mollie, moved to Oklahoma City.

Unexpected Fallout

To our surprise and dismay, however, we soon discovered that several of our older kids felt that we had abandoned them. To this day, this realization breaks my heart. It simply never occurred to us that anyone would feel that way. Each of our kids was so into their own life and busy schedule that we'd assumed they didn't really need (or want) us close by. Stunned, we faced the music—we had a family full of adult kids who felt disappointed and hurt by our choice to move our nest away from Indiana, the only home our blended family had ever known.

What happened next was just as stunning. As we attempted to work with the feelings of each of the kids, intending to heal any sense of abandonment, one by one, some of our older kids packed up and moved to Oklahoma City. And not only did they move to Oklahoma City, they also joined us in our small and simple home, which quickly became cramped and complicated.

Then, late one night, I had severe pain and tightness in my chest. Worried I was having a heart attack, Don called an ambulance, and I was rushed to the hospital, where they promptly ran all sorts of tests. Eventually the heart doctor came into my room to discuss the results.

"I have all good news," he announced. "Not only is your heart okay, it's in incredible shape."

Don and I breathed a sigh of relief, then asked the obvious. "Then what caused the symptoms?"

"Well, a panic attack can present similarly to a heart attack. May I ask, is there anything in your life right now causing a lot of stress?"

I thought about how to express briefly how I was feeling—not only closed in but like I was losing my inner voice again, disappearing into myself.

I explained our recent move to Oklahoma City, how that had deeply hurt our grown kids, how some of them had moved out to Oklahoma City, and how the new simple life we'd established had disappeared.

"Well," he replied, "that pretty much sums up a whole lot of stress."

Self-Talk

No one needed to tell me what my next step had to be. I could see it clearly. So off I went to some new counseling sessions. One of my biggest fears, I had learned earlier about myself, is being misunderstood. Discovering that my children—who were the delight of my heart—felt hurt, disappointed, and abandoned by "my" decision to move (even though Don and I had decided together, I felt the self-blame and shame) caused such pain that it had triggered a new slew of destructive self-talk.

It was your choice, your voice, which sent you moving away from Indiana. No wonder all the kids felt abandoned. How selfish you are. That's why you should never use your voice. It only causes hurt and pain.

Fortunately, with the help of the counselor and Don's wise and steady influence, I was able to quiet that self-talk with some truth: *Just because, when I used my voice, my adult kids felt hurt by my decision doesn't mean that my decision was wrong. My motives were not to hurt or abandon. Not everyone will always agree with my choices, and that's okay. It doesn't make me wrong. And it certainly doesn't mean that I should stifle my voice.* This was a huge breakthrough for me. In fact, I am still learning this lesson. I can't allow the fear that others may have a different point of view keep me from expressing my voice.

New Creations

We now have had five weddings in our beautifully blended family— blending even more loved ones into the fold. What an honor that is! Each wedding has been unique and has reflected the personalities of our kids. To be transparent with you, we're still learning how to be a healthy blended family when it comes to sharing major events like weddings, funerals, and hospitalizations that involve the other parents of our kids.

Don and I have noticed that we both tend to step back a bit when John is around, or when the memory of Don's ex-wife, Michelle (whom we lost a few years back), is powerful, not wanting to diminish the time and love our kids share and have shared with their other parents. We don't want to step on toes. And we notice that our kids seem to do the same—to step back. The result so far seems just a little sad, as if we haven't yet found a way to naturally experience the full breadth of emotional bonds we share—to embrace the joyous celebration or grieve the heartbreaking loss—when the full "extended" family members are present or are missed. Don and I have agreed to stretch ourselves in this area and to grow in wisdom as we experience such times. The blending of a family, we are discovering, goes on for decades, and that is okay. Just as in any family relationship—not just blended families—there is always growing to do.

I realized one way my voice is challenged during such major, full-family events is that the old voices return and shout into my ear. *If you hadn't made such a mess of things, this wouldn't be an awkward moment right now.* And, *It's your fault there is tension in this moment.* And, *You really are a lousy person and no one really wants you in their lives. They are just pretending.* And perhaps the loudest lying voice of all: *You've been kidding yourself to think that there can be healing. Nothing is healed. It's all an illusion.* In such moments, I entertain the idea that my life is a sham, that I am worthless, and that I never should have asserted my voice in the first place.

Oh, how easy it is to spiral down into self-doubt and God-doubt, to lose sight of all the wondrous healing God has already done. I have found, too, that when we are under this kind of stress, it is so easy to revert to unhealthy patterns of behavior, because there is false comfort in the old and familiar.

In the Old Testament, God rescued the Israelites from captivity and slavery through Moses. They celebrated their new normal. But then the going got tough, and the people reverted to their old worship of idols and longed for Egypt and slavery once again. I suppose they were oddly comforted by the familiar, so much so that they lost sight of where they were headed—to the Promised Land.

In times of great stress or major transition, I find myself relating to those freed Israelites so much. I've learned to recognize now when that backward draw is happening. I see when I am letting my voice fade away or gravitating toward pushing it down with food. I must then choose to silence the old voices with truth, invite the new normal front and center, recognize God's work in the midst of it, and celebrate his good work. At such times, I quote 2 Corinthians 5:17: "Therefore, if anyone is in Christ, the new creation has come: The old has gone, the new is here!"

Yes! I am the Lord's. You are the Lord's! We are his new creations, and we can live in that victory!

Therefore, when our nest is moved, when changes and transitions and losses and celebrations come our way, we need not fear that our newfound voices will falter or fail. We can recognize the warning signs. We can choose to silence our old voices, and we can victoriously coax our new voices out from hiding to front and center where they belong. We can stand on the truth of God's Word found in the apostle Paul's letter to the Philippians: "Being confident of this, that he who began a good work in you will carry it on to completion until the day of Christ Jesus" (1:6).

Discovering Your Voice

Use the following questions to think about some major transitions you have faced or are facing now.

- How have your major transitions affected the use of your voice?
- What negative self-talk is a red flag to you that you are reverting to less healthy, old, familiar ways of using, or not using, your voice?
- What are some of the ways God has nurtured and grown your voice? Think on those things and celebrate what God has begun in you and will complete.

When you have a wilderness moment, meditate on Isaiah 40:3. How will you prepare the way for the Lord?

> In the wilderness prepare
> the way for the Lord;
> make straight in the desert
> a highway for our God.

CHAPTER SIXTEEN

Forever Grateful

Recently, I came across a rudimentary picture I drew during my dark days of despair and brokenness. It was a simple stick figure, but none of the joints were connected. The arms didn't quite touch the body, and neither did the legs nor the head. In the center of the stick body, I had drawn a broken heart. I remember only too well what I was feeling when I drew it—I felt torn apart in every direction.

I remember that during those days, when I performed for an audience or interacted with them after a concert, it actually felt like they were *taking* a piece of me. The only place where I felt whole was within my music. It was the only voice I had. So, sad as this sounds, during those lowest of days, I resented my audience. It seemed they were *taking* my performances from me; I was using up the only voice I had, leaving less and less of me behind. I felt for a while that, with each concert, I became weaker and more voiceless. Hollow, wounded, broken, and believing myself to be damaged goods, I suffered in silence with my injured identity, afraid I was unworthy of love or value.

That was then.

The Voice

This is now: Today, if asked to draw a picture of myself, I would draw a stick figure connected from head to toe—a figure with a full, overflowing heart, arms outstretched with a gift in hand to give away, and a face with mouth open in speech and song pouring out to the world. I picture myself *giving* the music and my stories to the audience. What a stark contrast. The whole and healed Sandi Patty (notice the correct spelling!) who emerged from years of blending a family and years with Women of Faith now believes that her inner voice is as powerful as her singing voice—both effective tools to communicate God's unconditional love to the world.

As I've illustrated in the previous chapters, God brought me step by step from voicelessness to a fullness of voice. He brought me to a place where I came to truly know that he loves—and even likes—me, sees me, and keeps me safe in his arms. I understand now that he is changing me into a new creation, that I am enough. I am a work in progress that God was, and is, completing. I discovered that my voice is worth hearing, that I am worth the changes I wanted to make. And finally, I now realize that no matter how many stanzas of my life song I've sung, I still have more to sing. When I put all of that together, this is what I see: the song of my life tells the story of God's love.

Through the adventure of my career—the building days, the glory days, the painful days, the healing days, and now the celebration days—I've learned to love the chance to use my voice, in song and in words, to share about God's faithfulness, grace, mercy, and love. How ironic that more than thirty years ago, when arenas sold out with fifteen to twenty thousand people wanting to hear what I had to say, I didn't feel I had anything *worthy* to say. I was too busy pretending that life was perfect, that my marriage was perfect, and that being a young mom while having a busy career was perfect. I used so much energy trying to hold up walls that kept people out so they wouldn't know the truth.

Once I stopped trying so hard to project those illusions, I realized that it was so much easier just to be real. Risky, yes, but worth the risk. Now the truth is that there are fewer people listening to what I have to say, but I feel that now, more than ever, I have something of *importance* to say. For when I look out over an audience, and when I think on the many thousands who have gathered over the years to hear me sing, my heart is full to overflowing with the message that I want to sing and speak into every one of those lives:

You are loved and liked by Almighty God.

You are seen.

You are safe.

You are a new creation.

You are enough.

Your voice is worth hearing.

You are worth the change you want to make.

And as long as you are on this side of heaven, no matter how many stanzas of life you already have sung, you have more stanzas yet to sing!

The Tour to Say Thank You

I've now been traveling and singing professionally for more than thirty-five years.

The world of opera says that a woman's vocal prime is between the ages of forty-five and sixty. I have stepped over the latter end of that spectrum. We've all seen athletes who were once at the top of their game and of whom we now think, *Oh, man, they should have retired a long time ago.* I was determined not to be that kind of musician. I always want to be respectful of the art form.

So in 2015, I went to my management team and said, "It's time to think about retirement." I explained that retiring from a music career isn't the same as retiring from a nine-to-five job. You can't quite give a thirty-day notice and off you go. We needed to make a plan for the next couple of years. I explained that I wanted one last tour to say thank you to the people who have come alongside me on this crazy music-career journey. They had come to the concerts and listened to the CDs, albums, cassettes, and, yes, even eight-tracks. They had stood in long lines to tell me how God had spoken to their hearts through my songs. I was thankful for the spiritual impact of this ministry God gave me, and I realized that God had used that audience to minister to me as well. I wanted them to know how thankful I am to them.

So we put together a plan for a final tour. It needed a name, and I said, "We can call it anything except a finale or a farewell tour." I wasn't done singing; I was just done touring. For all those reasons, we decided to call it the *Forever Grateful* tour. And so we spent the better part of eighteen months—throughout 2016 and well into 2017—on the road traveling to city after city and church after church simply saying thank you through music. What an honor.

I've had people say, "Are you going to have a farewell tour number two and number three, like other artists do?" Nope! This is it. It seems I've been on the road all my life. And it's time to step off that road and away from singing full time. Traveling on a bus or a plane day after day feels much different to a sixty-plus-year-old body than to a thirty-plus-year-old body. It's just hard. Although I have loved the work and singing and meeting and ministering to people, the traveling and the "bounce back" are just harder the older you get.

Does this mean that my singing days are over? No, but my touring days are. I still have it in me to do occasional concerts and special events, and I now have a richer message than ever. I want my audiences to discover how to listen for God's voice in all the milestones and challenges of life so they will find their own voices and grow in their identities and abilities to express who they are, who they were created to be.

The Realization of a Dream

So, what now? I have always wanted to teach. Teaching has been my dream ever since elementary school. Now I am honored to be artist in residence at our church in Oklahoma City, Oklahoma. Don and I have called Crossings Community Church home for the past eight years. (Don is on staff as one of the music pastors, and he leads our chapel service.) I get to be part of the fabric of everything that happens music-wise at our church. Honestly, I think music is one of God's best creations. He just kind of outdid himself with music. It's everywhere. All around us. And I have the privilege to play a part in that.

I get to work with our vocal teams, and I get to, dare I say it, teach. I teach some music, and I teach the biblical perspective of worship and how God calls us to be our best and to bring our best. I get to encourage and engage audiences. I also get to speak to a Sunday school class of young parents because now I'm *not* that young parent. I get to walk into that Sunday school class and give those young parents a standing ovation because they made it to church today. I know that's a big deal.

In addition, I get to encourage the women in my life whom I am privileged to mentor in this season.

If it has taken all the stories of my life to bring me to this season, then it has been worth it. I'm not proud of some of my stories (as you now understand!), but while they can't be rewritten, God can reframe them for his good.

I am able to freely share that, guess what, marriage is hard. It's worth it, but it's hard. Raising kids, at any age, is hard. Family is hard. Life is just hard sometimes. But God is in the midst of the eternity of the hard days just as he is in the midst of the eternity of the good days. I have been more challenged and encouraged over the years by those who don't pretend to have it all together, those who speak from a place of authenticity. It is for that reason that I share the not-so-pretty chapters of my story. Not so that I can keep wearing the shame but so that I can offer someone hope that this isn't the end of the song. That they aren't in this alone. That we need each other. That when we share our stories with one another, we can find power and healing in community.

I think back to Mrs. Dominic saying, "We are going to find *that* voice." I've now spent a good deal of my life finding my voice. People like Mrs. Dominic, the Women of Faith women, my friends in our church small group, and especially my family—these are people who helped draw that voice out of me. Memories of their words and support continue to call out that voice. And I speak it and sing it wherever God places me in a position of influence.

So I may not be singing as much as I have done for the past thirty-five years, and I may not be traveling as much (except to see the grandkids), but I still have something to say, and I treasure every opportunity I have to share about this amazing God of mine. I step freely right into the center of that circle. Whether it's having coffee with a friend going through a divorce, or leading music in our church on Sunday morning, I do have some things to share that I've learned over the years. And it is my gift to give. I really do love how that feels.

For all those things and more, I am indeed forever grateful.

As I finished up the *Forever Grateful* tour, one thing happened just about every single night, and I never, ever tired of it. I would finish the concert with "We Shall Behold Him." As people responded by standing and applauding, it gave me a chance to acknowledge the band and Veritas (an amazing group of five gentlemen who sing so well they are like five Josh Grobans in one group), and then of course to thank my family. The band and Veritas would go offstage, and our family would remain to sing a cappella "It Is Well with My Soul." Then the family would exit, and I would have one last moment to sing my heart to the audience. It was just me and the piano. I sang a song that Nichole Nordeman and I wrote—"Forever Grateful." It truly expressed my gratitude and thankfulness to God, for without his love and mercy, none of life makes sense. But the song also expressed my heartfelt gratitude to the audience, so many of whom had been with me since the beginning.

After I finished the last song, often with tears in my eyes, I would walk silently offstage, quite emotional. And there my husband would be waiting for me. He would hug me and hold me just for a second. And then he would say, "Sandi, I see you, and I am so glad you have found your voice."

Discovering Your Voice

God has done so much for each of us. Use these questions to stimulate an attitude of thanksgiving and praise for his good gifts:

- Name some of the people who have helped you find and use your voice.
- Reflect on how you have been a help to others in finding their voices.
- Pray, asking God to reveal who may need your help to find and use their voice.

Of course, as we use our voices and encourage others to find and use theirs, our greatest calling, as Deuteronomy 30:19–20 says, is to listen to God's voice and hold fast to him.

> Now choose life, so that you and your children may live and that you may love the Lord your God, listen to his **voice**, and hold fast to him.

CHAPTER SEVENTEEN

God's Song

Finding my voice and growing in the confidence to use it has ushered me into a wondrous season. But nothing outweighs the wonder of hearing God's voice more clearly than ever as I listen for it—through his Word and through his people. There are a few verses in the book of Zephaniah that I love because they paint such a beautiful image of one way that God uses his voice. Given my lifelong love of music, I think you will see why I love these verses so.

> Sing, Daughter Zion;
>> shout aloud, Israel!
> Be glad and rejoice with all your heart,
>> Daughter Jerusalem!

> The Lord your God is with you,
>> the Mighty Warrior who saves.
> He will take great delight in you;
>> in his love he will no longer rebuke you,
>> but will rejoice over you with singing.
>> —*Zephaniah 3:14, 17*

The Voice

How dear to me that in verse 14, Jerusalem is personified as God's *daughter,* and she is urged to sing. I love to let those words echo in my mind. *Sing, daughter, sing!* And then in verse 17, we find an even more powerful image as God takes such great delight in his people that he rejoices over us with singing! Just imagine, God singing over you as he celebrates you. His love for you and me is so great that he bursts into song!

As I teach and mentor others, I want to be an echo of God's voice as he delights in and rejoices over those he loves. Just as I step into the young-parents Sunday school class and give those parents a standing ovation, I want to be intentional about applauding others by communicating God's unconditional love and outpouring of affection. In the same way, when I have the privilege to work with my church's vocal teams, I can do my best to inspire them—not simply to perfect their vocal skills but to spiritually engage with the messages they are proclaiming in song—with the messages of God's love and truth. I remind them to approach every performance prayerfully, lifting their audience up to the throne and helping them to experience God's majesty and power and love through the music. As believers— even those who can't sing—we all can use our voices to encourage and inspire one another. This means approaching each day, each encounter, with the mindset and determination to do just that.

Perhaps the very best place to practice using our voices is with our loved ones—those closest to us. For me, of course, that means my rather large family—my husband, eight children and their spouses, and three (so far) grandkids. But don't let my example throw you if you are single or have a smaller family. The principle is the same: As we use our voices for God with those with whom we interact regularly, our voices grow stronger and clearer and more intentional.

We grow into the habit of reflecting God's "song" over us, a habit that will naturally spill over to others whom God brings into our lives.

Still Feathering the Nest

I like the image of using my voice to feather my nest. Don and I have found ourselves in a new normal—empty nesters for good. All the kids are adults and living their own lives, out of the house. The funny thing is, I think the kids worry about our being alone, just the two of us.

"Poor parents," they seem to worry. "They must be so sad and lonely."

Can I be honest? It's *awesome.* We can go to a movie anytime we want. We go out with friends more often, and we can even snuggle in for the evening right after *Wheel of Fortune.* It really is a fun season for the two of us. When we got married, we didn't have a "just the two of us" season. For most couples, that usually happens before the kids arrive. But we did it backward, so we are making the most of it.

Having said this, I discovered that it wasn't as easy to shift into empty-nest mode as I'd expected. We were so used to having our lives revolve around all the kids' activities. As they moved away and into their own lives, we had more unscheduled time. We had to learn how to use our voices in this new empty space. And Don and I use our voices *very* differently.

I am very much an introvert. Most people don't realize that because they see me onstage, where I've learned how to use my extrovert self. But offstage, and with groups of friends or in family gatherings, I prefer to be a little more introspective. I'm quiet. In my head, I am very busy. (I even sleep busy! My mind is often going a thousand miles an hour as I climb into bed. When I wake up, I often remember my dreams.) My mind is always going, but what does Don hear when I'm in that mode? Silence. I have had to learn to speak up and say what I'm thinking or feeling and never expect Don to read my mind.

Don, on the other hand, is a full-on, full-steam-ahead extrovert. The more people the better. Life is just one big party. And words—oh my, does he use words! Extroverts seem to have many more words than introverts do. (The truth is introverts have as many words, but we keep them in our heads.) Let me just emphasize this—extroverts use *a lot* of words. And by *a lot* I mean ALLLLLLOOOOOOTTTTTT. Everything introverts are thinking or feeling internally, extroverts are saying out loud, often as fast as they are thinking it. Don said one time, "It's not that I talk a lot. I'm just thinking out loud." That's a funny way to look at it, but I guess that's true.

The problem comes when introverts and extroverts need to recover. Introverts recover by becoming hermits for a bit. Totally getting quiet and alone. Extroverts recover by being with more people and using even *more* words. (How is this even possible? I wonder.) So how, exactly, do introverts and extroverts relax and recover in the same room?

One of the things Don and I have learned to do is understand each other's personality type. Sometimes, extroverts just need to talk. Now, here's the shocker—they don't necessarily need anyone to listen to them. They just, in essence, need a body there to talk to. But my personality type always wants to fix whatever is wrong. So I've learned to say, with my big girl voice, "Don, do you need me to really lean in and listen, or do you just want to talk?"

A lot of times he'll say, "Oh, I just want to talk." And then I can feel a little relief in my spirit that I don't have to fix what he's talking about.

So then I say, "Talk away."

Then there are times when I want to talk, but I don't want to talk if there isn't going to be time to really finish the conversation, so I'll wait. When I begin talking, Don will interject something (extroverts just can't help themselves), and I'll say, "Hold it. I'm not done talking."

Sometimes he'll say, "Oh, I thought you paused," to which I reply, "I was just breathing."

If I'm the fixer, Don is the encourager. And then some! We call him Tigger, for Don is not just the guy who sees the glass half full. He'll say, "Wait, there's only one glass? I see thousands." Sometimes, when I need to speak my mind about something hard or something I'm struggling with, Don will go into encouragement mode. I used to hear that as a *"shut up and stop talking"* mode before I knew better.

Now I will gently say to him, "I'm gonna stop you right there. For the next two minutes, all I need from you is, 'Oh, honey,' or, 'I can't believe that.'" I don't need him to fix it. I just need him to be part of my process to uncover my voice. And he does a beautiful job. There are times that I'll just kind of go off on something, and he knows (now!) just to get out of the way and listen. And then he'll very kindly, and with great affirmation, say, "You know, baby, when you used to feel like you couldn't speak your mind and didn't feel like you had a voice? Well, I just want you to know, you've uncovered it. I hear you. I see you. You've got this, baby."

All this is to say, allow me to offer you some advice. If you are going to use your voice more, especially with loved ones, read up on your personality types. Take some personality tests like the Myers-Briggs or read up on the Enneagram. You'll learn so much about how better to communicate and not communicate. For Don and me, this has been an effective way for both of us to find and use our new voices.

I am continuing to learn what it means to sing into the lives of my eight adult children. Sometimes, I have discovered, the best voice to use is my listening voice, which requires time and silence, yet shouts love, acceptance, and value. To simply *be* there, to really hear their hearts, to hug, and to affirm—these are "notes" that my voice can sing into their lives. And it's worth it to learn those notes—to take voice lessons and stretch and practice.

When it comes to grandparenting, Don and I have a hard act to follow, because my parents are the best grandparents ever. They both were part of our "village" that helped us raise all those kids. So even before we had grandkids, Don and I talked about what kind of grandparents we wanted to be. One word that frequently comes to mind today, and was modeled by our parents, is the word *available*. That's honestly a challenging word because we don't live near all our grandkids. Our family is rather spread out all over the US. But we are available for Facetime and for babysitting when the parents need a getaway.

The other word that describes what we want to offer to our grandkids is *time*. We have the luxury that when we are with our grandkids, we don't have to multitask a job or run errands—the kinds of things that young parents have to do. We can just be there, available with our time.

We also decided that we would work with our kids and not against them. As young parents, they try to put a schedule and routine in place, and we don't want to be "those" grandparents who mess everything up when the kids are with them. Now, of course, we are likely going to stretch the routine and the schedule a bit, because we are grandparents and we've earned it. But we want to be helpful, not detrimental. I have many friends who are grandparents, and they say that when they have the kids, all the rules go out the window. That's just not our approach, even though we do stretch the routine a bit. Mostly, we believe that as long as the grandkids want to spend time with us, then we must be doing something right. We must be singing a song they love to hear.

Recently, the entire family was together for Thanksgiving. It was wonderful. All, hmm, let me count, eighteen of us. After dinner, the adult kids and spouses wanted to go grab dessert, so Popi (Don) and I offered to put the grandkids to bed. We had been given the sweetest gift of a gingerbread house that had caught four-year-old Thatcher's eye. He kept asking if we could open it and eat it. I finally quietly said to him that as soon as everyone left and the younger grandkids were in bed, he and Popi and I could open it and eat a bit of it, and then we could begin what has become a favorite family tradition—super wind down. Basically we get in our jammies, grab our favorite blanket, turn all the lights off, and watch a movie until we can't keep our eyes open.

Thatcher immediately announced to the rest of the family, "Hey, we need you guys to get out of here so me and Popi and Nani can start our super wind down." And once they all left, we did indeed open up that gingerbread house, and Thatcher proudly ate the door.

Don and I love using our Nani and Popi voices—voices of fun and togetherness, of affirmation and encouragement, and above all, of love. And when we think about it, aren't these the voices we want to sing to every child of God who comes through our lives? When we echo God's song in our lives, when we take delight in what he has done in us and for us and through us, we can't help but be glad and rejoice with *all* our hearts and voices.

Discovering Your Voice

As we are wrapping up this journey together, I find myself praying for you, the reader. I pray that you have heard the voice of God "singing" over you in this book. May you know his unconditional love for you and his delight in you as his child. I pray that, with God's voice as your anchor, you are able to find your own voice, that it is growing in strength and confidence, and that it increasingly reflects the voice of God to others. May you now use your new voice to sing a new song to the Lord. Sing God's song with him. The song of love.

There are so many beautiful Scriptures to meditate on that will help you find the words for your new song. I've chosen Psalm 98:1–6 here, for these verses are filled with the music of heaven. Read them aloud. Take your time. May they be your proclamation—the words of God's song, sung in your voice.

> Sing to the Lord a new song,
>> for he has done marvelous things;
> his right hand and his holy arm
>> have worked salvation for him.
> The Lord has made his salvation known
>> and revealed his righteousness to the nations.
> He has remembered his love
>> and his faithfulness to Israel;
> all the ends of the earth have seen
>> the salvation of our God.

The Voice

Shout for joy to the LORD, all the earth,
    burst into jubilant song with music;
make music to the LORD with the harp,
    with the harp and the sound of singing,
with trumpets and the blast of the ram's horn—
    shout for joy before the LORD, the King.

Epilogue

"Sandi," my doctor said one day while I was writing this book, "the good news is that you don't have any nodules on your vocal cords. The bad news is that they are swollen. I'm putting you on twenty-one days of voice rest."

Wait. What? I wanted to laugh out loud and say, "But you don't understand. I *have* to use my voice. I've just learned *how* to use it!" You know what I mean? It was one of those personal funny moments. To think that the doctor was saying I couldn't use my voice precisely when I was telling the world I'd finally found it! How ironic while writing a book titled, of all things, *The Voice.* Just too funny. You can't make up this stuff!

As I stifled the urge to laugh, I wanted to say, "Doctor, I don't think that is going to happen." But I knew better. It needed to happen. My vocal cords were tired. I had used them a lot in the last year and a half as we marched our way across the country with the *Forever Grateful* tour. To be honest, it wasn't just my vocal cords that were tired; I was tired all over.

My doctor (who was familiar with my music through the years) went on to say, "You are like an Olympic athlete. You have to work with your vocal cords and not against them." I understood his point. There is a way the vocal cords are meant to work, and they, like muscles in our body, need time to relax, rest, and recover. Just as athletes talk about recovery time after a game or a workout, singers, too, need recovery time.

There are different levels of vocal rest, and I was to progress through all three over the twenty-one days. One is complete silence. Another is gentle talking and gentle singing. Think of that like someone going to physical therapy after knee surgery or a shoulder injury. You don't immobilize your vocal cords but gently talk and gently *hmmm*. Then there is the last level when someone skilled guides you through vocal exercises to test the cords' strength and durability by singing higher notes and longer phrases. The point of each of these levels of vocal rest is to restore the voice to its greatest performance level, just as any kind of rest is meant to restore you and prepare you to be active once again.

The funny thing is, I don't know how to actively rest. Rest feels lazy to me. But rest, for recovery and health, is vital. I suppose that's true for our entire being and not just our vocal cords. Body, mind, and spirit all require rest.

Sabbath Rest

Rest is probably way more important than we realize. After all, God ordained rest. Even he rested on the seventh day. There is a Sabbath meant for rest.

I had a counselor stop me dead in my tracks one day when I was going on and on about how tired I was and how no one understood and blah, blah, blah. He simply said, "I hear all that. So let me ask you. When is *your* Sabbath?" I didn't have an answer. Those who work in the church on Sunday have to find another day to rest, regroup, and recover. My performances were quite often on weekends, so I needed to learn to do the same.

My husband, Don, has the awesome privilege of leading our chapel service at our church, a service that is traditional in music selections and in liturgy. As Don has studied the church's historical liturgy this year, he has shared with me what he has been learning about the Jewish Sabbath. Jewish people *prepare* for Sabbath. They don't wake up on a Saturday ready to celebrate Sabbath. Their Sabbath begins at sundown the evening before and goes to sundown the following day. They follow many customs to ready themselves for the Sabbath. (My favorite is that they sing a song praising the woman of the house for all the work she has done over the past week. Wouldn't that be nice?) They prepare by slowing down the evening before and then waking to the day ready to celebrate and remember what the Sabbath means. They anticipate the Sabbath and step into it for the purpose of health, reflection, and joy.

I am learning in this new season of my life that rest isn't a passive escape from activity. Rather, it *is* an activity—the activity of rest. This may not make sense in your head, but it does in mine. I have to plan to rest. I have to plan to recover. This embodies the idea, for me, that rest purposes me *toward* something, not *away* from something. It does not thwart my purpose but carries me toward it.

It helped me to think of my twenty-one days of vocal rest not as recovery *from* something but as a restoration *toward* something. And I realized that this perspective is why I am not dreading retirement.

I'm anticipating it with joy. I am preparing for it instead of resenting that the time has come. The *Forever Grateful* tour, for me, was kind of like the evening preparation before the Sabbath. Welcoming and anticipating what is to come, while being grateful for what has been.

God has commanded the Sabbath for our benefit, that we should rest, recover, and restore. We can give and give and give only so much until nothing is left. Then we can run on empty only so long. We have to stop and allow God to refill our spirits in the way that only he can—through his Word, through communion with other believers, and through time being quiet, listening for his voice.

Sometimes we must quiet our own voices to listen for his.

Where Shame and Savior Meet

I am grateful for my silence during this period of vocal rest. It makes my voice, and all it can communicate, so much sweeter. And I discovered something in the special communion time of silence with my Lord. I've learned that having and using my voice really has little to do with talking or singing. Those are simply outward expressions of my inward self. My voice, in which I now have confidence, comes from deep within, where my shame and my Savior meet. This is the deepest place from which my voice now speaks.

I began this book with the little story of my singing "Jesus Loves Me" in the voices of others. How fitting now to return to the simple truths that

> Jesus loves me, this I know,
> for the Bible tells me so.

Little ones to him belong.

They are weak but he is strong.

Yes, Jesus loves me.

Yes, Jesus loves me.

Yes, Jesus loves me.

The Bible tells me so.

This little song has truly been one of the cornerstone songs of my life. It has become my heritage as a child of God. I have a few friends who, how shall I say this, are just really smart. They have PhDs and all kinds of other letters after their names, and they have worked hard to earn those letters. I asked one of my friends what it is like to research and prepare a doctoral thesis. She said to me something that rings true in this season of my life. She said, "The more degrees you get, the more you study about less and less content. What you study goes much deeper in one area."

This reminds me of a saying that I love: *"The older I get, the more I've learned. And the more I've learned, the less I know. But what I know, I really, really know."* And this is why I love the simplicity of the words of "Jesus Loves Me." Because *this* I know! And I know it more deeply each day that passes.

Honestly, this is the cornerstone of our faith. It is the foundation upon which all other things make sense in our lives. It is how we get the clock set correctly. It is the lens through which we learn to see everything else. If we don't get that basic understanding, we miss it all. I'm so glad that I have learned *not* to miss it.

Now, however, after examining the journey of my voice, I realize that in his love for me, God *knows* me fully. And so that precious little love song has been beautifully and redemptively reframed for me.

> Jesus loves me,
> this I know!
> Jesus *knows* me,
> *this* I love!

He knows you, too! And he loves the sound of your voice!

Acknowledgments

It still remains a bit ironic for me that this book is titled *The Voice*. As you have discovered in these pages, my voice was hard for me to find. But I continue to find it, and I am so grateful for those along my journey who have been my champions and my balcony people (which is still one of the greatest images I've ever read that describes those people in our lives who cheer us on—thank you Joyce Landorf).

First and foremost—and I promise I'm not trying to sound like an award winner—I thank my Lord and Savior, and my friend, Jesus. Truly, I have come to love Jesus and his word so much. I finally believe that he *does* love me. He is so *for* me. And learning to walk in the light of that truth has enabled me to find my words and speak my voice.

I do not know what this life would look like without my family. We have a unique voice that we continue to learn to speak corporately as a family. I think it's because we have given each other permission and a safe space to speak our individual voices. I adore each one of you, and you have truly been the wind under my wings. Now it's your turn to fly, and I'm right there in *your* balcony.

A very special thank-you to my best friend, partner in life, truth speaker, best hugger ever, and the hottest grandpa on the planet, my hubby, Don. For everything and nothing—this is us! (FYI, we had that phrase *long* before the TV show—just sayin'.)

Beyond words, I send the most heartfelt thank-you to the team at Atkins Entertainment and the Anderson Group. You all breathe life into and put feet on these crazy dreams we've had all these years. Thank you especially to Mike Atkins and Anna Trent—visionaries extraordinaire.

Thank you to our church, Crossings Community Church, for giving us a safe and soft place to fall into God's grace. Thank you for walking with us into this incredible new beginning chapter.

Thank you Esther and the Fedd Agency team for being a great champion for this project.

To Cindy Lambert—thank you (although you clearly can say those words much more eloquently than I can) for putting voice to my voice. You are a master architect of the heart.

And finally to the amazing full-circle family of Zondervan. Thank you Sandy Vander Zicht for your incredible leadership and for choosing my voice. Thank you Brian Phipps for your insightful editorial excellence. Thank you Tom Dean, Bridgette Brooks, and the wonderful marketing team for doing what you do with such creativity and intentionality. Thank you David Morris for being involved so personally. I am so grateful to the entire team at Zondervan. Your caring teamwork has made this all possible.

Thank you, to *you!* Wherever you are, wherever you sit at this moment, I thank *you* for being willing to listen to my voice. I pray this book has encouraged your own voice.